THE CREDIBLE SING MACHINE
Volume I

Part 1: How it Works
Part 2: Open for Inventory

Maurice L. Allison

UNIVERSITY
PRESS OF
AMERICA

LANHAM • NEW YORK • LONDON

Copyright © 1986 by

University Press of America,® Inc.

4720 Boston Way
Lanham, MD 20706

3 Henrietta Street
London WC2E 8LU England

Library of Congress Cataloging in Publication Data

Allison, Maurice L.
    The credible sing machine.

    Contents: v. 1. How it works. Open for inventory—
v. 2. How to train. Melodic vocalization.
    1. Singing—Instruction and study.   I. Title.
MT820.A48   1986   784.9'32   85-26610
ISBN 0-8191-5200-5 (pbk. : alk. paper : v. 1)
ISBN 0-8191-5201-3 (pbk. : alk. paper : v. 2)

All University Press of America books are produced on acid-free
paper which exceeds the minimum standards set by the National
Historical Publications and Records Commission.

THE CREDIBLE SING MACHINE
Volume I

Part 1: How It Works

Maurice L. Allison

To

Addie Elizabeth Borders Allison, My Mother,
Who introduced me to Music,

And

Charles A. Woodbury, My Teacher and Prime Catalyst,
Who left me a glimmer of Hope,
A measure of Discontent.

I celebrate all those acousticians, physiologists and pedagogues who have sought vocal truth and shared their findings.

My thanks to Rose Marie Spivacke, Professor Emeritus, University of Maryland, for reading the early manuscript and providing the wise counsel and encouragement which persuaded me to continue the task.

I am indebted to Rosemary Steeg, distinguished Washington Metropolitan Area voice teacher, for reading the (later) manuscript and providing valuable advice, and for the continuum of open dialogue and support from both Rosemary and Bruce Steeg, noted pianist/conductor.

To Linden McIlvaine, outstanding educator and Music Specialist of the Prince George's County (Maryland) Public Schools, my gratitude for his reading of the manuscript and subsequent helpful response, and for his continued dialogue and devotion to vocal pedagogy for the student singer.

To the multitude of music teachers of the Prince George's County Public Schools who were subjected to persistent vocal dialogue, my thanks for their tolerance and their often helpful responses.

I thank Michael Cordovana, Professor and Chairman of the Voice Department of the Catholic University of America, for providing a major arena for the testing of the Credible Sing Machine, and for his courageous support of an unproved body of concepts.

To the students of the voice classes of the Catholic University of America, who applied the concepts to their voices, and by so doing provided essential input to the development of the training procedures for the Credible Sing Machine, a large measure of thanks.

FOREWORD

As a public school supervisor of vocal and general music (grades
7-12), I looked forward to the summer curriculum workshop of 1974, because it marked my first serious attention to _vocal_ music after years
of concentrated effort on the _general_ music curriculum.

The writing team was carefully screened and selected from many
applicants to include both elementary (grades K-6) and secondary (grades
7-12) gifted and skilled vocal music teachers. The long awaited ses-
sions began and, as we warmed up our respective skills in the exercise
of educational jargon, a vague suspicion grew to the sure knowledge
that WE COULD NOT COMMUNICATE VOICE! (But....surely you knew that.)

I, therefore, in that summer of 1974, resolved that I would find
out how the voice works and seek ways to communicate vocal technique
to those beautiful people who have brought wonderful musical experiences
to singers, but who lack the knowledge prerequisite to the actual and
necessary training of voice.

I have, in the more than eight years since the inauguration of my
vocal obsession, sought to accomplish this mammoth task by the extensive reading of the works of those who have also sought vocal truth
and have dared to print their findings; by engaging in persistent dialogue with those who were willing to look with me beyond the somewhat
mystical veil of vocal pedagogy; and, perhaps most important, by teaching to young and old, amateur and professional, ordinary and gifted,
functional and dysfunctional, the body of concepts and behaviours which
are offered herein as the Credible Sing Machine.

October 22, 1982
Maurice L. Allison
Adelphi, Maryland

PREFACE
                     AN INCREDIBLE SING MACHINE

        The incredibility of the vocal teaching profession was perhaps
best articulated by Victor Alexander Fields, who in 1947 listed twenty-
one causes of confusion in the vocal profession and some twenty-three

---

        Victor Alexander Fields, Training the Singing Voice. New York:
King's Crown Press, 1947, pp. 3-8.

---

years later succinctly restated the problem in a "Review of the Literature on Vocal Registers":

                "We draw the conclusion from a survey of vocal
                literature that the theory of registration is in
                controversy, as is nearly every aspect of vocal tech-
                nique; that definitions are vague and contradictory;
                that authors disagree as to the nature and existence
                of this phenomenon. The action of registration is no
                where clearly explained and the exact causes remain
                undecided."

        Victor Alexander Fields, "Review of the Literature on Vocal Reg-
isters", The NATS Bulletin, No. 26, 1970, pp. 37-39.

        Little has occured in subsequent years to prompt revision of Field's
accurate assessment. Voice pedagogy has been and is even now incredible,
or in the strictest sense of the word....unbelieveable.

        One thing is clear, the voice works in accordance with the laws of
nature as revealed by the scientific community and supported by universal
agreement.

        It follows that the voice, being a totally human sound producing
machine, works within those functional parameters defined by the science
of physiology.

        Finally, until someone can bring to vocal pedagogy a method which
combines the sciences of acoustics and physiology and present techniques
which make possible the identification of the individual voice capacity
and potential, we have no viable system of voice management....

            W E   H A V E   N O   V O C A L   P E D A G O G Y.

"DESCRIBE YOUR VOICE."

Well, uh . . . .

Sometimes I can HIT
a . . . .

It's never been what
you would call a very
strong . . . .

I've been told by my
friends that it's
not . . . .

I sang first soprano
in my high school
chorus, but . . . . .

My first college
teacher told me I
was a mezzo soprano,
but . . . .

My current teacher
says I should train
as a Spinto . . . . .

I can't seem to sing
pianissimo without
breathiness . . . . .

My voice seems to
tire quickly . . . . .

We have agreed on very little concerning vocal technique in general and voice registration in particular. This has been confirmed by the vague responses of hundreds of voice students and teachers who have been asked to

"D E S C R I B E   Y O U R   V O I C E."

Until we are able to define the boundaries of our voices we cannot effectively teach people to develop and maintain them. Our pedagogy is unreliable without a viable concept of voice registration.

To effectively use the voice as a vehicle for the communication of that which we call music we must have a pedagogy which obeys the natural laws as we know them and conforms to the limits of human tissues.

In essence the MUSICIAN who would be a VOCALIST must become also part ACOUSTICIAN and part PHYSIOLOGIST. Only then can there be candidates for the high designation of VOICE MANAGER.

NOMENCLATURE
OF THE
CREDIBLE SING MACHINE

I confess to a degree of preoccupation with words. I enjoy them.
It is to my mind a most positive liking for one who wishes to communicate something as important as a credible sing machine.

I delight in humor which derives from play with words. The verse
of Ogden Nash is a source of pleasure for me, especially when, finding
no suitable word for a rhyme, he alters an existing one or coins (sometimes called "corns") one for the occasion. A favorite comes to mind
from "The Wasp" in which the rhyme for prodigality was of course
"waspitality."

Ogden Nash, The Pocket Book of Ogden Nash. New York: Pocket
Books, Inc., 1962, p. 162.

When existing vocal nomenclature seems to be inappropriate, I offer
an alternative. When the traditionally used term is known to be inac-
curate and in the educational sense "myth-leading" (now you know me), I
have felt an urgency to suggest an option. I plead guilty to a certain
inconsistency in that I retain such obvious misnomers (oldies but good-
ies) as falsetto, which is most certainly "reallo", and vocal cords,
which would seem to catagorize the voice as a stringed instrument. I
do so because the acoustically and physiologically appropriate alterna-
tives, secondary mode voice and vocal ligaments connote a certain pom-
posity which I would avoid . . . . from time to time.

My base motive in the development of a new nomenclature for the
Credible Sing Machine was to increase the effectiveness of that communication which we call vocal pedagogy, with sincere thanks to those who
before me did likewise in their search for vocal truth.

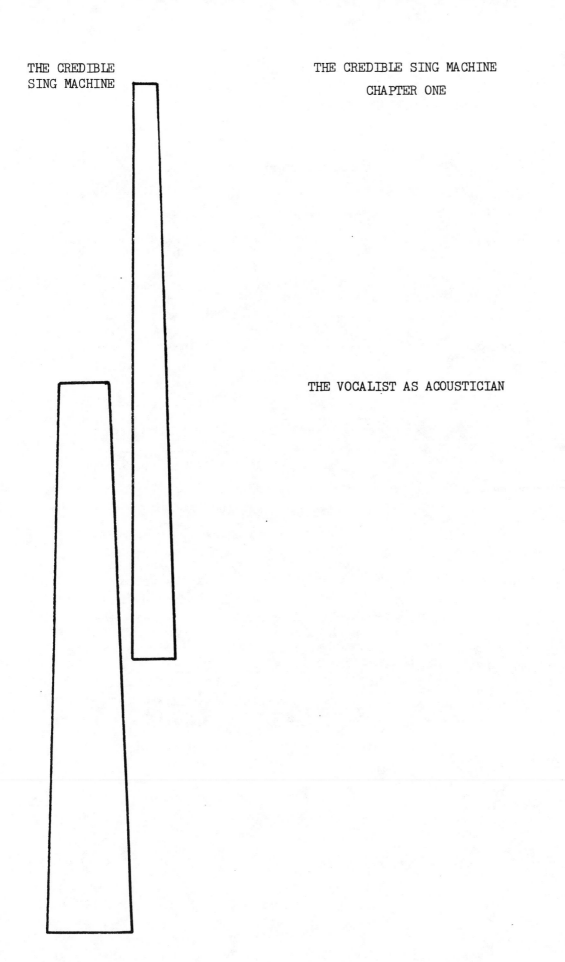

THE VOCALIST AS ACOUSTICIAN

THE KEYNOTE

B^b Clarinet	D^3
Bass Clarinet	D^2
Alto Saxophone	D^{b3}
Tenor Saxophone	A^{b2}
Baritone Saxophone	D^{b2}
Oboe	B^{b3}
Bassoon	B^{b1}
*Trumpet	E^3
*French Horn	B^1
*Trombone	E^2
*Tuba	F^1

Violin:
$$G^3 \quad D^4 \quad A^4 \quad E^5$$

Viola:
$$C^3 \quad G^3 \quad D^4 \quad A^4$$

Violincello:
$$C^2 \quad G^2 \quad D^3 \quad A^3$$

Double Bass:
$$E^1 \quad A^1 \quad D^2 \quad G^2$$

Soprano Voices:
$$D^4 \quad C\#^4 \quad C^4 \quad B^3$$

Alto Voices:
$$B^{b3} \quad A^3 \quad A^{b3} \quad G^3$$

Tenor Voices:
$$D^3 \quad C\#^3 \quad C^3 \quad B^2$$

Bass Voices:
$$B^{b2} \quad A^2 \quad A^{b2} \quad G^2$$

Note: The keynotes, or lowest fundamental pitches, are given in concert pitch. The brasses are asterisked to indicate a substituted, practical keynote.

My teacher and prime catylist in the search for vocal credibility, Dr. Charles A. Woodbury (1896-1960), in his voice class at Florida Southern College in 1952, stressed the importance of a practical application of scientific principles to voice teaching, stating that:

> "We must accept as fact that every instrument, whether made by God or by man is pitched to a certain keynote . . . so also is the human voice pitched to one or another key."

Charles A. Woodbury, Handbook for Choral Directors. Lakeland, Florida: Florida Southern College, 1951.

This viewpoint was supported by the scientific community and stated concisely by Clarence E. Bennett, who wrote:

> "All bodies have natural frequencies of vibration, depending on their masses, their geometric characteristics, and the manner in which they are set into vibration."

Clarence E. Bennett, Physics Without Mathematics. New York: Barnes and Noble, 1949, 1970, p. 61.

These statements constitute the rationale for the concept of voice registration which I will share with you as

THE CREDIBLE SING MACHINE.

Readers who lack fundamental knowledge of acoustics or who feel the need for a refresher course in the scientific study of sound may benefit from the perusal of one or more of the concise articles to be found in most standard music reference works. If time is available make a major investment by studying one of the many texts on the subject.

My introduction to acoustics was Wilmer T. Bartholomew's "Acoustics of Music" which disappeared from my shelf many years ago, it's influence lingering behind. I have listed some works which have been especially helpful to me generally and in the preparation of this work. Please do not read further in "The Vocalist As Acoustician" until you have some basic understanding of acoustics.

Bennett, Clarance E. Physics Without Mathematics (College Outline Series) New York: Barnes & Noble, 1970 Revised.

    Chapter V: Elastic Considerations (pp. 59-63)
    Chapter VI: Waves and Sound (pp. 72-84)

Benade, Arthur H. Horns, Strings & Harmony (Science Study Series) New York: Anchor Books, 1960.

Olson, Harry F. Music, Physics and Engineering. New York: Dover, 1967 Second Edition.

    Chapter 1: Sound Waves (pp. 1-24)
    Chapter 5: Musical Instruments (pp. 108-200)
    Chapter 6: Characteristics of Musical Instruments (pp. 201-241)

Scientific American (Readings from). The Physics of Music. San Francisco: W.H. Freeman and Company, 1978.

Magie, William Francis. A Source Book in Physics. Cambridge, Massachusetts: Harvard University Press, 1963.

    Sound (pp. 115-116)

Bartholomew, Wilmer T. Acoustics of Music. New York: Prentice-Hall, 1942.

To dramatize the consistent behaviour of all musical instruments
with regard to the harmonic overtone system, sometimes called the
"scale of nature", I have created a comparative study of voice and
other musical instruments. A portion of that study is included here
as an introduction in acoustical terms to my concept of how a credible sing machine works.

As a preliminary to the study please read the clarifications of
the language of Bennett's statement which is the framework for the
study. I repeat the statement for the sake of clarity.

> ALL BODIES HAVE NATURAL PERIODS, OR FREQUENCIES
> OF VIBRATION DEPENDING ON THEIR MASSES, THEIR GEOMET-
> RIC CHARACTERISTICS, AND THE MANNER IN WHICH THEY ARE
> SET IN VIBRATION.

CLARIFICATIONS

1. Bodies   - All matter, since all matter vibrates contin-
                   ually.

2. Vibration   - A movement back and forth through a point of
                   equilibrium, OR ANY PERIODIC PROCESS.

3. Period   - Time required for one vibration.

4. Frequency   - Number of vibrations occuring in one second.

5. Mass   - Properties of matter which determine it's re-
                   sistance to change.

6. Geometric   - Physical arrangement of matter.
   characteristics

The application of Bennett's statement to matter specifically
arranged for the expression of music calls for the substitution of
musical instruments for bodies and requires further clarification
based on personal experience and observation of the instruments.

Now let us test the statement in a variety of ways, applying
each part of the statement to instruments having universally recog-
nized registration. Oh yes, one other.... V O I C E.

"ALL BODIES...."

    All musical instruments....

"ALL BODIES HAVE NATURAL FREQUENCIES OF VIBRATION...."

    All musical instruments have a lowest fundamental
pitch....

"ALL BODIES HAVE NATURAL FREQUENCIES OF VIBRATION...."

    All musical instruments have a lowest fundamental
pitch plus a series of other pitches produced by
pitch regulatory devices....

"....DEPENDING ON THEIR GEOMETRIC CHARACTERISTICS...."

    All musical instruments which have similar geomet-
ric characteristics will excite the harmonic series
in similar sequence....

"....DEPENDING ON THEIR MANNER OF VIBRATIONAL ACTIVATION...."

    All musical instruments which have similar geomet-
ric characteristics and similar manner of vibrational activation will have similar registration....

"....DEPENDING ON THEIR MASSES."

    All musical instruments which have similar geomet-
ric characteristics and similar manner of vibrational activation, but are of dissimilar mass will
have different frequency ranges.

All musical instruments....

CONOPHONES

Conophones, the saxophones and oboes, are equipped with conical engines; set into motion by single or double reed vibrators; and powered by the breath.

Sample Instrument - SAXOPHONES

CYLINDROPHONES

Cylindrophones, the clarinets, are equipped with cylindrical engines; set into motion by single reed vibrators; and powered by the breath.

Sample Instrument - CLARINETS

CYLINDRO-CONOPHONES

Cylindro-conophones, the brasses, are equipped with HYBRID engines, cylindrical and conical; set into motion by the vibrating lips in a cup-shaped mouthpiece; and powered by the breath.

Sample Instrument - TRUMPET in B-FLAT

FIBROPHONES

Fibrophones, the stringed instruments, are equipped with one or more uniform (diameter) string engines; set into motion by the vibration of the string; and powered by plucking, striking, or bowing.

Sample Instrument - VIOLIN STRING in D^4

LIGAMENTOPHONES

Ligamentophones, human voices, are equipped with ligamental engines, the vocal cords; set into motion by the vibration (periodic process) of the vocal cords; and powered by the breath.

Sample Instrument - SOPRANO in C^4

All musical instruments have a lowest fundamental pitch....

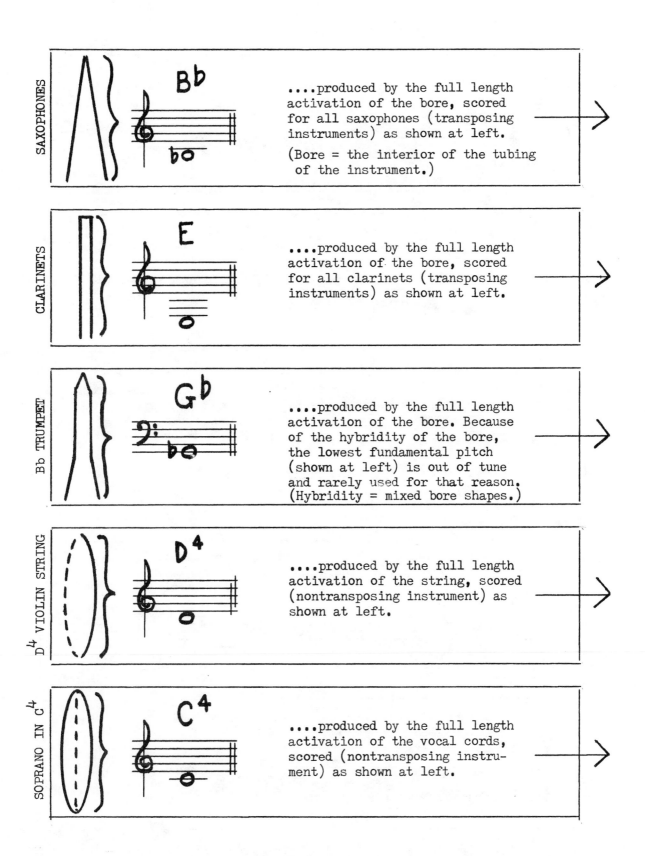

SAXOPHONES — Bb

....produced by the full length activation of the bore, scored for all saxophones (transposing instruments) as shown at left.

(Bore = the interior of the tubing of the instrument.)

CLARINETS — E

....produced by the full length activation of the bore, scored for all clarinets (transposing instruments) as shown at left.

Bb TRUMPET — Gb

....produced by the full length activation of the bore. Because of the hybridity of the bore, the lowest fundamental pitch (shown at left) is out of tune and rarely used for that reason. (Hybridity = mixed bore shapes.)

D^4 VIOLIN STRING — D^4

....produced by the full length activation of the string, scored (nontransposing instrument) as shown at left.

SOPRANO IN C^4 — C^4

....produced by the full length activation of the vocal cords, scored (nontransposing instrument) as shown at left.

All musical instruments have a **lowest** fundamental pitch plus a series of other fundamental pitches produced by pitch regulatory devices.

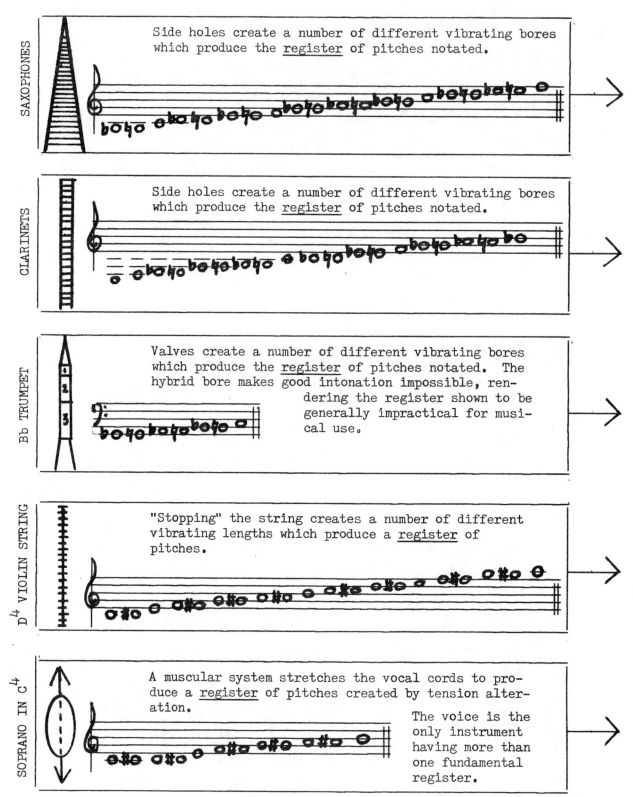

SAXOPHONES

Side holes create a number of different vibrating bores which produce the register of pitches notated.

CLARINETS

Side holes create a number of different vibrating bores which produce the register of pitches notated.

Bb TRUMPET

Valves create a number of different vibrating bores which produce the register of pitches notated. The hybrid bore makes good intonation impossible, rendering the register shown to be generally impractical for musical use.

D⁴ VIOLIN STRING

"Stopping" the string creates a number of different vibrating lengths which produce a register of pitches.

SOPRANO IN C⁴

A muscular system stretches the vocal cords to produce a register of pitches created by tension alteration.

The voice is the only instrument having more than one fundamental register.

All musical instruments which have similar geometric characteristics will excite the harmonic series in similar sequence.

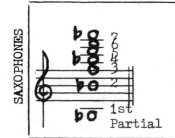

SAXOPHONES

All saxophones (conophones) exite the harmonic series in the sequence 1 2 3 4 etc. times
the lowest mode frequency. Each of the fundamental register pitches can be produced as the
<u>first</u> <u>partial</u> of a series of partials which
can be produced simultaneously.

(Partial = one harmonic. Similar to but more
appropriate than "overtone.")

CLARINETS

All clarinets (cylindrophones) excite the
harmonic series in the sequence 1 3 5 7 etc.
times the lowest mode frequency. Each of the
fundamental register pitches can be produced
as the <u>first</u> <u>partial</u> of a series of partials
which can be produced simultaneously.

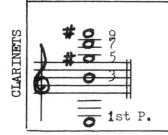

Bb TRUMPET

All brasses (cylindro-conophones) excite
the harmonic series in the sequence 1 2 3 4 etc.
times the lowest mode frequency. Each of the
fundamental register pitches can be produced
as the <u>first</u> <u>partial</u> of a series of partials
which can be produced simultaneously. (See
intonation statement on preceeding page.)

D⁴ VIOLIN STRING

All strings (uniform) excite the harmonic
series in the sequence 1 2 3 4 etc. times the
lowest mode frequency. Each of the fundamental
register pitches can be produced as the <u>first</u>
<u>partial</u> of a series of partials which can be
produced simultaneously.

SOPRANO IN C⁴

All voices excite the harmonic series in
the sequence 1 2 3 4 etc. times the lowest
mode frequency. Each of the fundamental register pitches can be produced as the <u>first</u>
<u>partial</u> of a series of partials which can be
produced simultaneously.

All musical instruments which have similar geometric character-istics and similar manner of vibrational activation will have similar registration.

SAXOPHONES	VIBRATOR Single Mechanical Reed	The single reed system of the saxophones is capable of eliciting a secondary mode register based on the 2nd partial (see preceeding page) plus a limited range of pitches in higher modes. Two "speaker holes" high in the bore facilitate upper register production.

CLARINETS	VIBRATOR Single Mechanical Reed	The single reed system of the clarinets is capable of eliciting secondary mode registers based on the 3rd and 5th partials (see preceeding page) plus a limited higher partial range. One "speaker hole" expedites production of these upper registers.

Bb TRUMPET	VIBRATOR Human Lips	The lips of the brass player are capable of eliciting secondary mode registers based on the 2nd, 3rd, 4th, 5th, 6th, 7th partials (see pre-ceeding page) and beyond by variation of tension. Remember, the fundamental register is out of tune and incomplete (without special devices) as only seven of the necessary twelve pitches can be pro-duced.

D⁴ VIOLIN STRING	VIBRATOR AND ENGINE Uniform String	Although harmonics (partials can be produced by a light touch at precise points on the string, the string is for all practical purposes a one register instrument. The alternative to regis-tration was to equip the stringed instrument with enough strings to create the desired range span.

SOPRANO IN C⁴	VIBRATOR AND ENGINE Vocal Cords	Vocal cords can by reduction and segmentation of the active length elicit up to three registers in fundamental mode and three in secondary mode based on the 1st, 2nd and 3rd partials (See pre-ceeding page).

All musical instruments which have similar geometric characteristics and similar manner of vibrational activation, but are of dissimilar mass will have different frequency ranges. (Concert pitch shown.)

"ALL BODIES...."

    All voices....

"ALL BODIES HAVE NATURAL FREQUENCIES OF VIBRATION...."

    All voices have a lowest fundamental pitch....

"ALL BODIES HAVE NATURAL FREQUENCIES OF VIBRATION...."

    All voices have a lowest fundamental pitch plus
    a series of other pitches produced by a pitch
    regulatory mechanism....

"....DEPENDING ON THEIR GEOMETRIC CHARACTERISTICS...."

    All voices, because they have similar geometric
    characteristics, will excite the harmonic series
    in similar sequence....

"....DEPENDING ON THEIR MANNER OF VIBRATIONAL ACTIVATION...."

    All voices, because they have similar geometric
    characteristics and similar manner of vibrational
    activation, will have similar registration....

"....DEPENDING ON THEIR MASSES."

    All voices, because they have similar geometric
    characteristics and similar manner of vibrational
    activation, but are of dissimilar mass will have
    different frequency (pitch) ranges.

THE VOCALIST AS PHYSIOLOGIST

A HUMAN MACHINE

The voice is a mechanical unit of the human body.

ENGINE

It has an engine, the VOCAL CORDS, which converts breath into sound waves.

POWER SOURCE

It's power source, the LUNG SYSTEM, fuels the engine, providing energy requirements for phonation.

AUXILIARY UNIT

An auxiliary unit, the PHARYNGES, the ORAL CAVITY, and the NASAL CAVITY, tempers the output of the engine in its role of RESONATOR while the malleable walls of the oral cavity create the role of ARTICULATOR, giving the voice the unique distinction of being the only linguistic musical instrument.

The physiologist is concerned with the function of voice. Once we have an acoustically sound (no pun intended) concept of voice registration we can ask important questions. If the vocal cords are indeed the engine of the voice, how do they work? What is their function?

The scientific community affirms the role of the vocal cords as the voice engine, citing the "breath passing between the two vocal cords in the larynx that vibrate to restrict and release the flow of air" as the voice is produced.

McGraw-Hill Encyclopedia of Science and Technology, 1971, p. 771.

The vocal cords ARE the engine. They are composed of highly elastic ligaments, which, being elastic, can recover from distortion by force. The force which adjusts the cords for a full range of musical expression is muscular force.

The Vocalist as Physiologist will explore the muscular movement and the elastic recovery of the vocal cords, the

ENGINE OF THE VOICE.

Many books have been designated A & P but in truth the emphasis has been on the parts, the anatomy, with precious little on the function, the physiology of voice.

I have supplied the names of muscles which <u>could</u> provide the motive force for the function of the vocal cords. I believe the list to be quite accurate, however, I totally endorse the CONCEPTS of vocal physiology here given.

I have been the beneficiary through both agreement and disagreement of the work of many who sought vocal truth in the area of anatomy and physiology. I recommend the perusal of the following listed works as a preliminary to continued reading of the Credible Sing Machine.

Saunders, William H. <u>The Larynx</u>. CIBA Pharmaceutical Company, Summit, New Jersey, 1964, pp. 67-69, Reprinted from Clinical Symposia, Volume 16, Number 3, 1964.

Introduction; Physiology of Phonation; Structure of the Larnyx.

Palmer, John M. <u>Anatomy for Speech and Hearing</u>. Second Edition. New York: Harper & Row, 1972, pp. 97-126.

Chapter 5: The Laryngeal Region (pp. 97-126)

Vennard, William. <u>Singing: the Mechanism and the Technic</u>. Revised edition, greatly enlarged. New York: Carl Fischer, 1967.

Chapter 4: Registration (pp. 52-79)

Appelman, D. Ralph. <u>The Science of Vocal Pedagogy (Theory and Application</u>. Bloomington, Indiana: Indiana University Press, 1964.

Chapter 3: Phonation: The Larnyx as a Biological-Biosocial Organ (pp. 41-102)

Fields, Victor Alexander. <u>Training the Singing Voice (An Analysis of the Working Concepts Contained in Recent Contributions to Vocal Pedagogy</u>). New York: King's Crown Press, 1947.

Chapter IV: Concepts of Phonation (pp. 98-128)

THE VOCAL ENGINE HOUSING
THE LARYNX

The larynx is the housing of the engine of the voice, the vocal cords. The larynx (LAH-RINX) is situated between the pharynx, above, and the trachea, below, just forward of the esophagus. Palmer uniquely described the larynx as an expansion of the respiratory airways to accomodate the "sliding doors", or vocal folds.

John M. Palmer, Anatomy for Speech and Hearing. New York: Harper & Row, 1972, Second Edition, p. 97.

In a physical sense the total pitch range of the voice could be referred to as the "neck" voice, because the production of all pitches occurs within the boundaries of the larynx.

The larynx is supported by one major bone, and includes five major cartilages, four of which are major components of the engine housing, the thyroid, the cricoid, and the (paired) arytenoids. (The fifth major cartilage, the epiglottis, is prominent in terms of resonance.) The major components of the vocal engine housing are reviewed individually as a preliminary to the introduction of the physiology of the vocal engine.

THE LARYNX

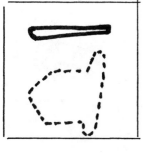

SUPERSTRUCTURE

The HYOID, an upsilon-shaped <u>bone</u>, supports the thyroid cartilage from above, providing an important stabilizing function.

FORWARD ENGINE MOUNT

The shield-shaped THYROID CARTILAGE provides the forward attachment for the vocal engine (cords) and is loosely attached to and is stabilized from below by the cricoid.

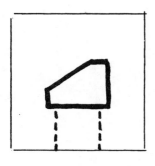

REAR ENGINE MOUNTS

The paired, ladle-shaped ARYTENOID CARTILAGES provide the rear attachments for the vocal engine. They are attached loosely to and are stabilized by the cricoid.

ENGINE BLOCK

The signet ring-shaped CRICOID CARTILAGE forms the base for the forward and rear engine mounts and is attached to the trachea below.

SUBSTRUCTURE

The TRACHEA or windpipe forms the lower attachment for the cricoid and provides the power line between the lungs and the vocal engine.

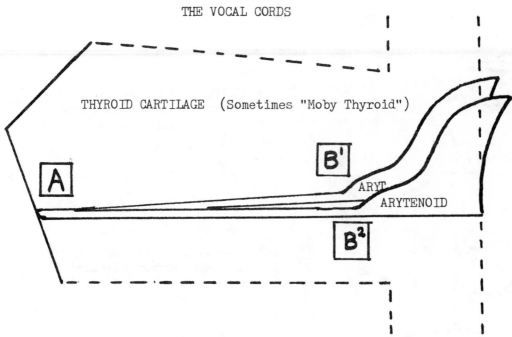

THYROID CARTILAGE (Sometimes "Moby Thyroid")

Called by many names, perhaps most commonly the misnomer
VOCAL CORDS, this engine of the sing machine is composed of two
elastic ligamental edges, shown above in their relationship to
the "engine mounts" or points of attachment to the laryngeal
housing.

 The anterior terminals of the vocal
cords are fixate (always joined) and
are called the anterior commissure.

 The posterior terminals of the vocal
cords are separate and can be ad-
justed in synchronized movement to
achieve phonation or respiration.

To demonstrate the physiology of the vocal cords I introduce
a new perspective, a conceptual approach to the function of the
engine of the Credible Sing Machine.

A SUPERIOR PERSPECTIVE

The anatomical description of the selected perspective for the introduction of the physiology of the vocal engine (nee <u>vocal</u> <u>cords</u>) is a

SUPERIOR,	(from above,
POSTERIOR-ANTERIOR	from back to front
SUPRA-LARYNGEAL	immediately above the larynx
TRANSVERSE	crosswise, horizontal
PLANE.	section.)

OR

A view of the cross section of the larynx from behind and above.

THE PROCEDURE

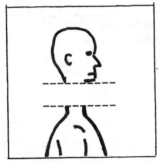

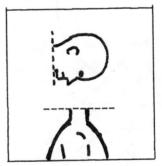

View with the mind's eye the careful detachment of your head at a point just above the larynx.

Now, in a detached manner, observe from above and behind the function of the vocal engine.

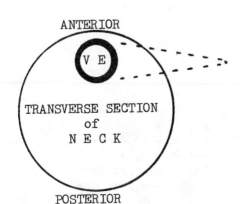

ANTERIOR

V E

TRANSVERSE SECTION
of
N E C K

POSTERIOR

THE VOICE ENGINE

Focus your "detached" retinae on that portion of the neck called the larynx for

A SUPERIOR PERSPECTIVE.

THE VOCAL CORDS
A SUPERIOR PERSPECTIVE

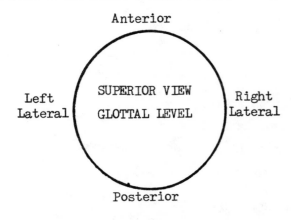

The physiology of the vocal cords will be shown as a superior view of the transverse plane at glottal level. This will permit you to think downward to your own level of voice production.

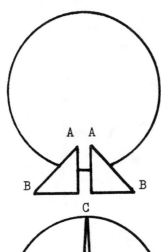

The arytenoid cartilages (see "Rear Engine Mounts") will be represented as two triangles with two vocal processes A , points of attachment of the vocal cords and two muscular processes B , points of attachment for some of the movers of the vocal cords.

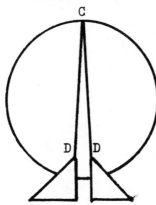

The vocal cords will be seen as two lines attached anteriorly in fixed adduction (always together) C and posteriorly to the vocal processes of the arytenoids D .

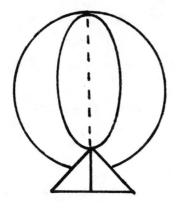

The vocal cords will be shown in various aspects to denote the expression of music. The vertical dotted line will indicate the midline, the oval lines reveal the displacement of the vocal cords during phonation.

THE VOCAL ENGINE AND IT'S MOVERS

Concept: To produce the full potential range of musical
            expression the vocal cords must be moved in a
            variety of ways.

ADDUCTION   -   Approximation

                            Separation

SEGMENTATION   -   Single Segment

                            Multiple Segment

VERTICAL PHASE   -   Latitudinal Thickening

                            Latitudinal Thinning

REDUCTION   -   Longitudinal Shortening

                            Longitudinal Lengthening

PITCH REGULATION   -   Lineal Stretching

                            Lineal Recovery

INTENSIFICATION   -   Lateral Stretching

                            Lateral Recovery

COMPRESSION   -   Approximation

                            Separation

PULSATION   -   Periodic Lineal Loosening

                            Periodic Lineal Recovery

Concept: Preliminary to voice production is the APPROXIMATION
of the vocal cords.

RESPIRATION

The posterior cricoarytenoid muscles
rotate the arytenoids to separate the
vocal cords for the breathing process.
The relaxation of the transverse interarytenoid permits added separation.

ADDUCTION PHASE ONE

The lateral cricoarytenoid muscles
rotate the arytenoids so that the vocal
cords are brought closer together than
in respiration.

ADDUCTION PHASE TWO

The transverse interarytenoid
muscle contracts to approximate the
vocal cords. This is the prephonation
posture.

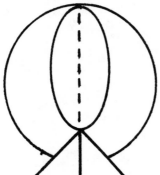

PHONATION

During phonation the muscles of
the ADDUCTION SYSTEM must provide the
coordinated function of anchoring the
vocal cords in the pitch regulatory
process.

Concept: Quality can be produced by the simultaneous
SEGMENTATION of the vocal cords.

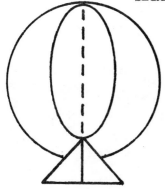

FIRST PARTIAL

The first partial is nonsegmented,
a fundamental mode frequency.... will
be stronger than segmented frequencies
.... will be heard as the pitch of a
complex sound.

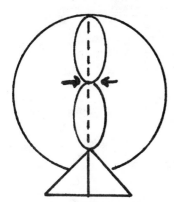

SECOND PARTIAL

The bisegmentation of the vocal
cords is a function of the vocalis
muscle with the cooperation of the
oblique interarytenoids (see "Vertical
Phase System").

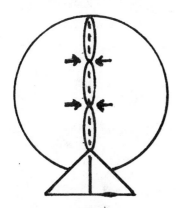

THIRD PARTIAL

The trisegmentation of the vocal
cords is a more complex function of
the vocalis and oblique interarytenoids providing for two nodes (points
of rest) and increased vertical phase
relationship.

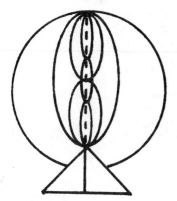

ALL TOGETHER NOW .... QUALITY

This base quality can now be con-
veyed to the RESONATOR SYSTEM for refinement and the conversion to language, a most sophisticated quality.

Concept: Two modes can be produced by the latitudinal
                      THICKENING (and THINNING) of the vocal cords.

Fundamental mode production is the simultaneous activation of
fundamental (single segment) and secondary (two or more segments)
vibrational modes by the vocal cords.

FUNDAMENTAL MODE

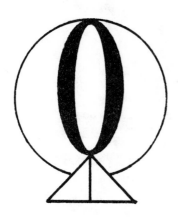

The transverse and oblique interarytenoid muscles cooperate to separate
the apices (tips) of the arytenoids so
that the vertical phase relationship of
the vocal cords is such that a relatively THICK portion is activated
throughout the vibrating length.

Secondary mode production is the production of a secondary (two
segments) vibrational mode without the activation of a fundamental
mode by the vocal cords.

SECONDARY MODE

The transverse and oblique interarytenoid muscles combine to bring together the apices of the arytenoids so
that the vertical phase relationship
of the vocal cords is such that a relatively THIN portion is activated
throughout the vibrating length. This
stance bypasses the potential fundamental mode and isolates the "overtone"
mode. (See the "Segmentation System,
Second Partial")

Concept: A dramatic range can be produced by the latitudinal
                  THICKENING (and THINNING) of the vocal cords. (See
                  "Modal Controls")

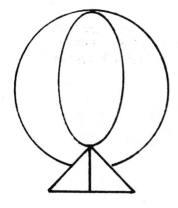

LYRIC

A lyric range of drama for a voice
is achieved by a <u>lesser degree of thick-
ness</u> than that of the optimal (see below).

OPTIMAL

The optimal dramatic level for a
voice is achieved by a <u>moderate degree
of thickness</u> of the vocal cords.

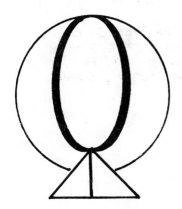

DRAMATIC

A dramatic range for a voice is
achieved by a <u>greater degree of thick-
ness</u> than that of the optimal (see above).

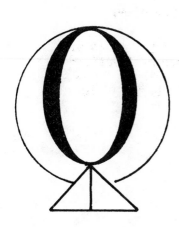

Concept: A series of registers can be produced by the longitudinal SHORTENING (and LENGTHENING) of the vocal
cords.

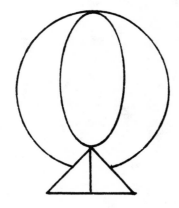

FULL LENGTH ACTIVATION

The lowest register is produced by
the full length vibration of the vocal
cords. Obviously, the reduction system
is not required.

HALF LENGTH ACTIVATION

A second (higher) register is produced as the _vocalis_ muscle functions
to deactivate the posterior half of the
vocal cords. (See "Segmentation, Second
Partial")

THIRD LENGTH ACTIVATION

A third (highest) register is produced as the _vocalis_ muscle deactivates
the posterior twothirds of the vocal
cords. (See "Segmentation, Third Partial")

MODE ONE

Concept: The registers produced by the Reduction System can
                      be activated in the fundamental mode.

ALPHA ONE

The Alpha One register is composed
of a series of pitches which include
the simultaneous production of the first,
second and possibly the third partials
(see "Segmentation") in full length activation.

BETA ONE

The Beta One register features a
series of pitches which include the
simultaneous production of the first,
second and possibly the third partials
(see "Segmentation") in half length
activation.

OMEGA ONE

The Omega One register consists
of a series of pitches which include
the simultaneous production of the
first, second and possibly the third
partials (see"Segmentation") in
third length activation.

Concept: The registers produced by the Reduction System can
be activated in the secondary mode.

ALPHA TWO

The Alpha Two register is composed
of a series of pitches, each consisting
of the second partial only in full
length activation. (See "Vertical Phase")

BETA TWO

The Beta Two register is made up
of a series of pitches, each consisting
of the isolated second partial in half
length activation. (See "Vertical
Phase")

OMEGA TWO

The Omega Two register is composed
of a series of pitches, each consisting
of the isolated second partial in third
length activation. (See "Vertical Phase")
(Theoretically possible, but impractical.)

Concept: A series of pitches can be produced within each
                  register by the lineal STRETCHING (and RECOVERY)
                  of the vocal cords.

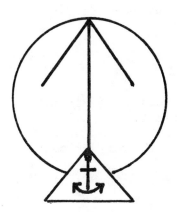

TO RAISE THE PITCH

The forward engine mount, the
thyroid cartilage, is pulled forward
by the cricothyroid muscles to
stretch the vocal cords and thus
raise the pitch. The rear engine
mounts, the arytenoids, anchor the
vocal cords through function of the
Adduction System.

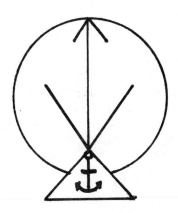

TO LOWER THE PITCH

The recovery of the vocal cords
is primarily accomplished by the
elastic factor of the cords, aided
by the stabilizing function of the
thyroarytenoid muscles. The crico-
thyroids continue reduced opposition
to facilitate recovery.

The antagonistic (yet cooperative) function of the STRETCHING
and RECOVERY subsystems is critical to the production of each pitch.

Concept: A range of loudness can be produced by the lateral
                        STRETCHING (and RECOVERY) of the vocal cords.

     As breath force of varying intensity is applied to the approxi-
mated vocal cords, they are activated in varying degrees of displacement to create a dynamic range. The resultant sound waves of differ-
ing amplitudes are heard as degrees of loudness.

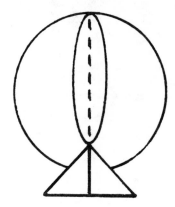

SOFT

     Soft singing is produced as minimal
breath force is expended to laterally
STRETCH the vocal cords. The softer the
dynamic level, the less the displacement.

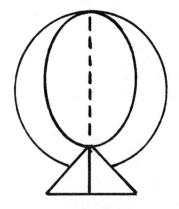

LOUD

     Loud singing requires the coordina-
ted function of all muscular systems
having pitch or quality responsibilities,
as maximal breath force is applied to
laterally STRETCH the vocal cords. The
louder the dynamic level, the greater the
displacement.

     The RECOVERY of vocal cords STRETCHED by breath force is accom-
plished by the elastic fibers which make up the cords.

Concept: An expressive range can be produced by the medial
                      COMPRESSING (and DECOMPRESSING) of the vocal cords.

VOCAL KALEIDOSCOPY

The Adduction System, I speaks to the prephonation function, the
rotation of and the pulling together of the vocal cords. The Adduction System, II concerns the _degree_ of this function, which creates
a wide range of nuance, a veritable kaleidoscopy of musical expression.

These often called vocal _colors_ have been given names such as,
mezza voce, _sotto voce_, _a voce piena_ and _voce di testa_. The names
have indicated that voice can be _full_, _half_, _head_, _middle_, _chest_,
subdued, and even _false_!

The reality is that only two modes of basic production are
available to the singer and they are fundamental mode voice (full)
and secondary mode voice (falsetto). All the rest are expression
within one of the modes achieved by alterations of the posterior
controls of the vocal cords. (Review "Adduction System, I; Vertical
Phase System et al")

The degree of approximation of the vocal cords for this expression ranges from _hypocompression_ to _hypercompression_, each extreme
having potentially deadly consequences for vocal tissues when
overused.

I have catagorized expressive indicators into five major units
of function.

Concept: Quiet, light expression is achieved by minimal
                        compression of the vocal cords.

| |
| CALMATO |
| DELICATO |
| DOLCE |
| LEGGIERO |
| LIEVO |
| MORBIDO |
| MORMORANDO |
| TENERAMENTE |
| TRANQUILLO |

These expressive indicators have in common
defining words quiet (soft) (5), delicate
(4) and others such as gentle, lightly,
calm, murmuring, easily, sweet, refined,
elegant and tenderly.

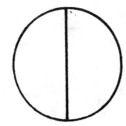

WEIGHT

Minimal weight requirements.
Vertical phase system in lyric attitude. Less than optimal weight.

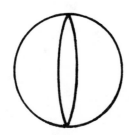

LOUDNESS

Minimal loudness requirements.
Intensification system in soft
activation.

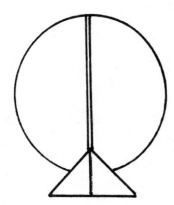

COMPRESSION

Minimal weight and loudness requirements are achieved by minimal
compression. (Accelerated singing
requires minimal compression.)

Concept: Smooth, graceful expression is achieved by moderate
                compression of the vocal cords.

AFFABILE
ELEGANTE
GARBATO
LISCIO
PIACEVOLE
P^LACIDO
SOAVE
VELLUTATO
VEZZOSO

These expressive indicators have in common
defining words <u>smooth</u> (6), <u>graceful</u> (4) and
others including <u>refined</u>, <u>elegant</u>, <u>flowingly</u>,
<u>tranquil</u> and <u>gentle</u>.

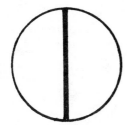

WEIGHT

Moderate weight requirement.
Vertical phase system in optimal
range.

LOUDNESS

Moderate loudness requirement.
Intensification system in medium
activation.

COMPRESSION

Moderate weight and loudness
requirements are achieved by moderate
compression.

Concept: Dignified, stately expression requires maximal
                    compression of the vocal cords.

| FASTOSO |
| GRANDIOSO |
| GRAVE |
| LARGAMENTE |
| POMPOSO |

These expressive indicators have in common
defining words <u>dignified</u> (4), <u>stately</u> (5),
and others such as <u>solemnly</u> and <u>broadly</u>.

WEIGHT

Considerable weight requirements.
Vertical phase system approaching
functional limits.

LOUDNESS

Substantial loudness requirements.
Intensification system in extensive
activation.

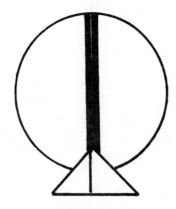

COMPRESSION

Maximal weight and loudness requirements are achieved by maximal
compression.

Concept: Vigorous expression is accomplished by maximum
                  compression of the vocal cords.

CON BRIO
CON FORZA
ENERGICO
FIERO
RISOLUTO
TONANTE

These expressive indicators have in common
the defining word <u>vigorous</u> (6) plus <u>bold</u>,
<u>firm</u>, <u>thundering</u>, <u>decisive</u>, <u>spirited</u> and
<u>with emphasis</u>.

WEIGHT

Utmost weight requirement.
Vertical phase system in extreme
dramatic posture.

LOUDNESS

Greatest loudness requirements.
Intensification system in extreme
activation.

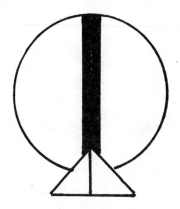

COMPRESSION

Maximum weight and loudness
requirements demand maximum compression.

Extensive singing in this part
of the expressive range often results
in hypercompression, a prime cause of
vocal cord pathology.

Concept: Mournful, plaintive expression requires subminimal
                  compression of the vocal cords.

CON DUOLO
FLEBILE
FUNERALE
LAGRIMOSO
LAMENTOSO
LUTTUOSO
MALINCONICO
MESTOSO
PIANGEVOLE
SOSPIRANDO

These expressive indicators have in common
the defining words mournful (6) and plaintive
(4), plus sighing, melancholy (2), sorrowful,
sad (3) and grieving.

WEIGHT

Maximum weight requirement.
Vertical phase system in dramatic
posture.

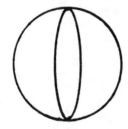

LOUDNESS

Minimal loudness requirement.
Intensification system in soft
activation.

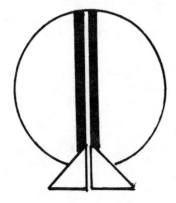

COMPRESSION

Maximum weight and minimal loudness
are achieved by subminimal compression.

Subminimal compression to express
pain requires the noise of leaking air
(breathiness) and requires a major
threat to coordinated voice production,
hypocompression.

Concept: A regular tonal pulse can be produced by periodic
                      tension variation of the vocal cords.

The mysterious neural pulse which relieves all muscles of the
body from the rigors of repeated like stimuli triggers the vocal
muscles (most likely the thyroarytenoids) to substantially delay the
onset of voice fatigue.

The comprehensive 1932 University of Iowa Studies in the Psychology of Music revealed that all great artists sing with this pulse,
commonly called the VIBRATO, about 95% of their production time.
Subsequent studies have indicated an even higher adherance to this
normal bodily function.

Carl E. Seashore, editor. The Vibrato, Volume 1, Studies in
the Psychology of Music, University of Iowa Studies. Iowa City,
Iowa: University of Iowa, 1932, p.351.

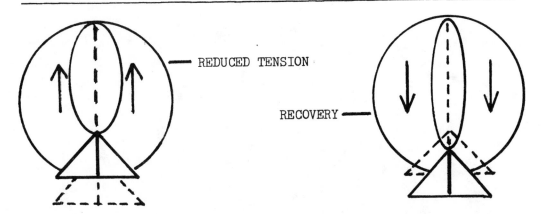

It seems likely to me that the anterior contraction of the
thyroarytenoids and the opposing contraction of the cricoarytenoids
and interarytenoids provide the tension variation necessary to enhance the function of the chief pitch regulation muscles, the crico-
thyroids. The pulse of tension variation creates an accompanying
pulse of intensification variation as displacement varies.

SUMMARY

THE PHYSIOLOGY OF A VOCAL SOUND

Before a musical vocal sound can be produced, the complex anatomy of the vocal engine must function in the following ways:

The <u>Adduction</u> <u>System</u> must approximate the vocal cords with the appropriate degree of compression for the expression indicated;

The <u>Segmentation</u> <u>System</u> must be set for the required quality package of partials;

The <u>Vertical</u> <u>Phase</u> <u>System</u> must activate the selected mode and degree of weight.

The <u>Reduction</u> <u>System</u> must provide the correct activating length for the chosen register and mode;

The <u>Pitch</u> <u>Regulation</u> <u>System</u> must apply the exact lineal stretch for the musical pitch;

The <u>Intensification</u> <u>System</u> must respond to the appropriate degree of breath pressure to achieve the desired loudness.

The <u>Pulsation</u> <u>System</u> must furnish the shock absorber protection for the total system.

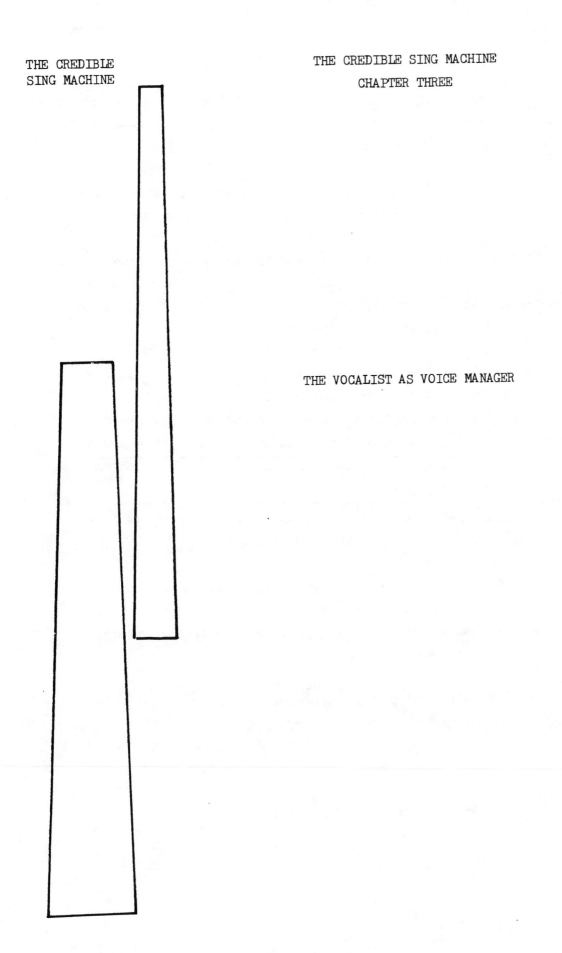

THE VOCALIST AS VOICE MANAGER

"The Vocalist as Acoustician" has through comparative registration given us strong support for the existence of an acoustically credible scheme of registration for the voice.

"The Vocalist as Physiologist" has described ways in which the vocal cords can be moved in order to fully express vocal music.

Now "The Vocalist as Voice Manager" has the task of orchestrating the aforesaid movements of the vocal cords in such a manner that the results will not only be aesthetically pleasing but will at the same time enhance the maintenance of the voice.

Paul Hume, the distinguished Washington Post critic, reminded us in his article "Game Plan for Disaster: The Right Singer in the Wrong Role" of the urgency for the selection of music within the boundaries of range and weight of the singer. Unfortunately many singers are

Paul Hume. "Game Plan for Disaster: The Right Singer in the Wrong Role", Washington Post, February 13, 1977.

uninformed (or misinformed) of either limit or the unmentioned limit of loudness, the third of the disaster areas.

The Credible Sing Machine to be a viable concept must reveal the extent within limits of each movement of the vocal engine. Perhaps the most important concept of voice management is that of realizing the limits of the vocal tissues.

With the acquisition of the concepts of elastic and muscular limits a new dimension of vocal pedagogy emerges :

THE VOICE MANAGER

Concept: To produce the full potential range of musical ex-
                pression the vocal cords must be moved in a variety
                of ways. The function must be accomplished within
                the limits of elastic tissues and muscular tissues.

ELASTIC LIMITS

All elastic matter has limits. To exceed the elastic limits of
a body is to risk loss of elasticity. Hooke's Law speaks to this
issue clearly. Within elastic limits stress is proportional to strain.
Vocal longevity depends upon the operation of the vocal cords within
musical limits which can be performed within the elastic limits of the
cords.

Since vocal cords have the ability only to recover from distortion
by force, the movers of the cords become important.... muscles.

MUSCULAR LIMITS

Striated muscles are the movers of the vocal cords. They are
capable of heavy work, but work best in moderation. They can work
for long periods of time, but require a warming up period as well
as periodic rest. They may be relatively inactive for a few days,
but thrive on regular work. Extended inactivity renders them in-
operable. To function efficiently they must be coordinated. The
development of strength must occur within the limits of coordination.

TRUISM

ALL MATTER HAS ELASTIC LIMITS

That everything has limits has been acknowledged through the years to be a truism .... and often overlooked in a vocal sense. Perhaps the most generally visible example of this self-sacrificial practice is found in sport, a prominent arena of competition.

When competition rears it's head all the efforts of preventive sports medicine come to naught when two or more superbly conditioned sprinters approach the tape neck and neck and their moment of truth arrives. What choice? Victory, recognition, adulation, remuneration.... or the ogre of defeat, obscurity, silence, loneliness.... or both. What price victory? Add to the gamble of simple overextension the risk of contact competition and the likelihood is increased that the price of success will be high as human systems collide in unpredictable force units.

A similar spirit of competition exists for the aspiring, though usually less visible, vocalist, with less spectacular results, but no less debilitating to the loser or short-term winner.

The vocalist, in order to climb the aesthetic peak, stimulate the adoration of a knowing audience, achieve the recognition of peers, and receive remuneration permitting the good life must do so within the elastic limits of the vocal cords. The musician (in us) and the vocalist (in us) must cooperate to choose a total program of vocal activity which is appropriate in terms of pitch, loudness and weight.

The athletic conditioner has no precise indicator of how far to move tissues. Often the limit is a feeling of discomfort or pain which probably indicates that the limit has already been exceeded.

The voice conditioner has also been without a precise indicator. To proceed further toward that acquisition we need a law, a scientific statement which has received universal acceptance.

(HOOKE'S) LAW

WITHIN THE ELASTIC LIMIT, STRESS IS PROPORTIONAL TO STRAIN.

Robert Hooke's concept of the elastic limit, now (having received universal acceptance) called "Hooke's Law" and a fundamental law of physics, was described by Bennett as follows:

"When a distortion is produced in a body by the application of force, the restoring force per unit of area (called stress), which is developed in all elastic bodies, is proportional to the fractional deformation (called strain) so long as the elastic limit is not exceeded. Thus, within the elastic limit, stress is proportional to strain."

Clarence E. Bennett. Physics Without Mathematics. New York: Barnes & Noble, 1970, p. 60.

When vocal ligaments are lineally stretched, laterally stretched, latitudinally thickened, or any combination of the three, the sum total of the distortion must be within the capacity of the tissues to recover without excessive stress. Thus we are limited in terms of pitch, loudness and weight to a precise range of function.

Within the appropriate range of function elastic tissues can be maintained. Without the limits function is reduced as elasticity is spent and an insidious progression often culminates in pathology of the vocal tissues as misuse elicits a physical alteration of vocal tissues.

What are these elusive boundaries for which vocalists and their pedagogues have searched throughout the history of musical voice? Patience. We first require a logical arrangement, a design, a delineation of the vocal limit.

THE SCALE OF NATURE
DELINEATOR OF THE ELASTIC LIMIT

The Vocalist as Acoustician (Chapter 1) knows that all musical instruments which have similar geometric characteristics will excite the harmonic series in similar, simultaneous sequence and that if the manner of vibrational activation is also similar they will have similar registration based on that same sequence.

TI^2 LI^2 LA^2 SI^2 SO^2	Ranges from the 3rd Harmonic to the pitch just below the 4th Harmonic.
THIRD HARMONIC	
FI^2 FA^2 MI^2 RI^2 RE^2 DI^2 DO^2	Ranges from the 2nd Harmonic to the pitch just below the next higher harmonic.
SECOND HARMONIC	
TI^1 LI^1 LA^1 SI^1 SO^1 FI^1 FA^1 MI^1 RI^1 RE^1 DI^1 DO^1	Ranges from the 1st Harmonic (the lowest correct pitch) to the pitch just below the next higher harmonic.
FIRST HARMONIC	

Vocal cords (like their cousins the strings and the cones) excite the harmonic series in the sequence one - two - three - etc. times the fundamental frequency of the voice (see "DO^1" the lowest pitch possible within elastic limits) and have fundamental registers based on the first three harmonics (as shown at left). This is clearly demonstrated in the registration of the young child and the early adolescent.

Adherance to the boundaries of the register is function within the elastic limit.

When each pitch within a register is produced within the limits of <u>loudness</u> and <u>weight</u> the production can be periodic or regular.

To dramatize the importance of function within the elastic limit we should explore production

WITHOUT THE ELASTIC LIMIT.

A remarkable event occurs when the vocal cords have been extended to the elastic limit and the vocalist orders the vocal muscles to take the cords beyond.

T H E Y   R E F U S E   T O   D O   S O!

In order for the vocalist to overextend the instrument, another system of muscles, generally called the extrinsic muscles of the larynx must effect an alteration of laryngeal posture, thus deviously (and perhaps dangerously) creating the required hyperextension or hypoextension of the vocal cords. This additional range of pitches, or weight, or loudness, or combination of the three is an example of hyperactive voice production.

It is not that the vocal muscles are necessarily unable to contract further to accomplish this indiscreet at best chore .... in the neural sense, they, being related to the vocal cords, simply choose not to injure a family member. These intrinsic vocal muscles are governed by the vocalist via the vegus, the tenth cranial nerve. The extrinsic invaders belong to another neural family which is more than willing to oblige the unwise vocalist in the quest for self-destruction of the vocal tissues.

This phenomenon provides a visual indicator of vocal overextension and makes possible a viable concept of internal posture of the engine of the Credible Sing Machine.

WITHOUT THE ELASTIC LIMIT
APERIODICITY, IRREGULARITY, NOISE

The response of the vocal engine to out of limits production can be perceived in terms of <u>acoustics</u>, <u>physiology</u> and <u>psychology</u>.

<u>Acoustical</u> <u>response</u>. Once the vocal cords are without the limit they cease to be producers of periodic waves. <u>Aperiodicity</u> becomes the norm.

<u>Physical</u> <u>response</u>. Aperiodicity is created by <u>irregularity</u> of function. When production is irregular the coordination of the vocal cords is reduced, with the result the abuse of delicate membraneous tissues.

<u>Psychological</u> <u>response</u>. Aperiodic waves created by irregular function of the vocal cords are perceived as <u>noise</u>.

To paraphrase Hooke's Law, "Within the elastic limit, vibrations are periodic, function is regular, and the result is perceived as <u>music</u>."

NOISE IS .... a disturbance
an obscurer of quality
the aesthetic block
a herald of hyperactivity
an aural indication of tissue destruction
a warning which must be heeded

Noise is described as a symptom of vocal hyperactivity, the chief cause of vocal problems.

The symptom will cease to exist only after the abuse, usually violation of the elastic limit, is removed. There are three manifestations of abuse which aid in the diagnostic process.

There are three major indicators of the exceeding of the elastic
limit of voice, the visual, the sensate and the aural.

1. The Visual Indicator

Production without the elastic limit is accompanied by
a change of posture which can be observed by the singer (mir-
ror) or teacher.

2. The Sensate Indicator

The singer who produces voice outside the limit must
develop awareness of the feeling elicited by overextension.
The singer should communicate the sensation to the teacher.

3. The Aural Indicator

The character of the sound changes when the elastic limit
is exceeded. The singer and teacher must acquire skills to
increase the perception of the sounds of vocal hyperactivity.

Now for the application of these diagnostic tools to the
individual components of a musical sound, pitch, weight and loudness.

Remember, there is also a limit to what can be accomplished
outside the elastic limit.

A TRIAD OF LIMITS

PITCH

WEIGHT

LOUDNESS

Posture for production within the limit places the vocal cords in
an optimal relationship. The horizontal aspect of the anterior and
posterior engine mounts must be appropriate, neither too high nor too
low with regard to the respective positions of the <u>thyroid</u> <u>cartilage</u>
(shown below) and the <u>arytenoids</u> situated superior to the <u>cricoid</u>
<u>cartilage</u>.

This posture must remain constant through the production of all
pitches, in all registers of each mode.

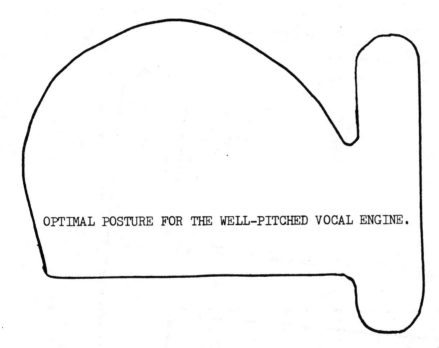

OPTIMAL POSTURE FOR THE WELL-PITCHED VOCAL ENGINE.

Incorrect posture for <u>breath</u> <u>management</u>, such as an inordinately
low rib cage posture, can depress the thyroid cartilage and thus interfere with production.

Incorrect posture of the velum in <u>resonation</u> <u>management</u> can alter
the resonance package and interfere with production.

The most dangerous posture is that which requires the cooperation
of the <u>extrinsic</u> <u>muscles</u> to tilt the thyroid cartilage to increase or
decrease tension on the vocal cords and produce a range of OVEREXTENSION.

Upward overextension occurs when pitches are produced <u>above</u> the limit of a register. It is a common practice of the limited registration vocalist who attempts to add to the range by devious means.

<u>Upward overextension is observable</u>. The posture change required to hypertense the vocal cords is accomplished by a technique somewhat akin to swallowing (a fact which sired the misnomer). The <u>hyoid bone</u> is caused to move in such a way as to tilt the <u>thyroid cartilage</u> forward and downward, rotating on it's lower attachment to the <u>cricoid cartilage</u>. This forward "thrust" adds tension to the cords and thus assists in the production of dangerous pitches.

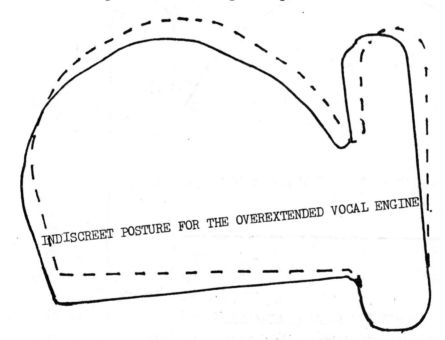

INDISCREET POSTURE FOR THE OVEREXTENDED VOCAL ENGINE

The behaviour required to achieve this indiscretion is quite simple and easy. It is merely a change in the posture of the jaw, observable as a <u>protrusion</u> (jutting) <u>of the jaw</u>.

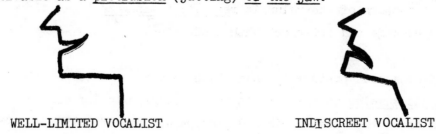

WELL-LIMITED VOCALIST   INDISCREET VOCALIST

Downward overextension occurs when pitches are produced <u>below</u> the limit of a register. This is a common practice of the choral singer having a (potential) soprano or tenor voice, yet electing to sing the alto or bass part.

<u>Downward</u> <u>overextension</u> <u>is</u> <u>observable</u>. The posture change required to hypotense the vocal cords is negotiated by the same "cast of characters" as in the previously described upward overextension except that the opposing muscles have dominance. The <u>hyoid</u> <u>bone</u> is moved so as to tilt the <u>thyroid</u> <u>cartilage</u> backward and upward, rotating on it's lower attachment to reduce tension on the cords and provide for the production of the heinous subfundamental pitches.

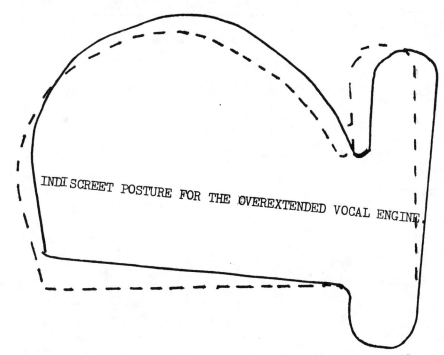

INDISCREET POSTURE FOR THE OVEREXTENDED VOCAL ENGINE

The behaviour required to achieve this range is easily accomplished and clearly observable. It is again a change in the posture of the jaw, observable as a turtle-like <u>retraction of the jaw</u>.

WELL-LIMITED VOCALIST   INDISCREET VOCALIST

WITHIN THE WEIGHT LIMIT
THE WELL-WEIGHTED VOICE

From the lower terminal pitch of a register to it's higher terminal pitch the geometry of the vocal cords changes .... from loose to taut .... from thick to thin .... from short to long.

As the geometry changes, so must the technique be allowed to conform, especially in terms of voice weight as the tissues lose thickness. In a physical sense, the technique does not change, however many singers add weight by changing the vertical phase relationship of the vocal cords as the pitch rises. This prompted pedagogues such as Mathilde Marchesi to instruct singers to "slightly close" the two highest notes of a register.

Mathilde Marchesi. Bel Canto: A Theoretical and Practical Vocal Method. New York: Dover, 1970, p. XV.

The internal posture or vertical phase relationship of the cords must remain at a moderate level throughout the range of the voice. (See "Vertical Phase System, II")

A cross-section of the cords shows them to be in a moderate range of activated depth.

Within the weight limit all pitches can be produced with a moderate degree of compression.

TI²	
LI²	
LA²	INCREASING
SI²	TAUTNESS THINNESS
SO²	LENGTH
FI²	
FA²	
MI²	
RI²	INCREASING
RE²	TAUTNESS
	THINNESS
DI²	LENGTH
DO²	
TI¹	
LI¹	
LA¹	
SI¹	
SO¹	
FI¹	
FA¹	INCREASING
	TAUTNESS
MI¹	THINNESS
RI¹	LENGTH
RE¹	
DI¹	
DO¹	

Whether it is called "belting or "bringing the chest up to the middle....or the head", the over-weighted voice is that which activates excessive amounts of tissue to create a <u>bigger</u> voice. This increased size has been referred to as <u>dark</u>, <u>dramatic</u>, <u>heavy</u> and even more vague titles.

Physically, as the cords are stretched and thinned for higher pitches, the <u>vertical</u> <u>phase</u> <u>system</u> rotates to bring additional tissues together for phonation. Within limits, this is a viable technique for musical expression; as a regular practice it is detrimental to the coordination of the vocal instrument.

The act of adding weight to the pitch can be sensed by the singer, but only after concepts of <u>weight</u> and <u>loudness</u> are clarified and isolated.

Over-weighting creates hyper-compression, the number one cause of vocal cord pathology.

TI^2	Vocal "obesity" decreases the function of the cords to the extent that often one or more of the upper registers are lost or produced only with undue force.
LI^2	
LA^2	
SI^2	
SO^2	
FI^2	
FA^2	
MI^2	
RI^2	
RE^2	
DI^2	
DO^2	
TI^1	
LI^1	
LA^1	
SI^1	
SO^1	INCREASING
FI^1	TAUTNESS
FA^1	THICKNESS
MI^1	LENGTH
RI^1	
RE^1	
DI^1	
DO^1	

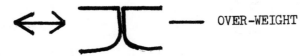

OVER-WEIGHT

APPROPRIATE WEIGHT

It has long been the practice, as in the Bel Canto vocalization the "messa di voce", to combine the increase or decrease of loudness with a similar change of weight. This is a valid musical expression, but there are times when the two must be separate and distinct and loudness must be altered without weight adjustment.

The practical (within limits) range of vocal loudness includes those degrees of amplitude, or lateral stretch, which can be produced within the capacity of the adduction, segmentation, reduction, pitch regulation, and vertical phase systems to work in coordination without hypercompression of the vocal cords.

The elastic limits of the vocal ligaments are then determined by the total demands of pitch, weight and loudness.

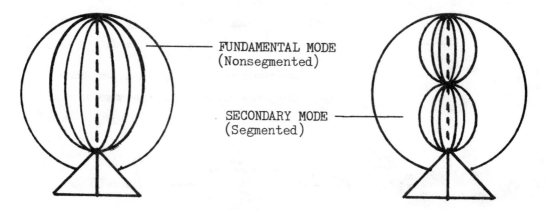

FUNDAMENTAL MODE
(Nonsegmented)

SECONDARY MODE
(Segmented)

Secondary voice (falsetto) production is limited to less than fundamental voice (full) production because of the nonfixate central node which gives way when the limit is exceeded and reverts back to fundamental production.

Literature which calls for extreme degrees of loudness (as symbolized by "ff", "fff" or even "ffff") need not pose a problem for the individual singer if the singer considers the loudest musical demand in terms of the individual limit.

When the loudness limit has been exceeded the resultant sequence occurs:

The muscular system abused by excessive power is the <u>adduction system</u> (see "Adduction System, I")

The lateral stress literally overpowers the <u>lateral cricoarytenoids</u>, pulling the vocal processes apart. The maintenance of pitch becomes difficult as the decreased stretch is heard as flatting of the pitch.

The posture for upward pitch overextension (see "Without the Pitch Limit") is one of the compensatory strategies.

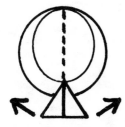

Another strategy is to increase the compression of the vocal cords at the vocal processes by added contraction of the <u>lateral cricoarytenoids</u>.

Unfortunately these actions combined only act to overpower the <u>transverse interarytenoid</u> muscle, creating a triangular opening between the arytenoids (commonly called the "mutational chink" because of it's occurance during adolescence) which allows air to escape unused for musical production.

The hypercompressed cords are now unable to operate in free vertical phase to produce <u>quality</u>.

The Triad of Limits has been presented as an "arpeggio" of limits, but in fact they must be managed as a <u>blend</u> of pitch, weight and loudness.

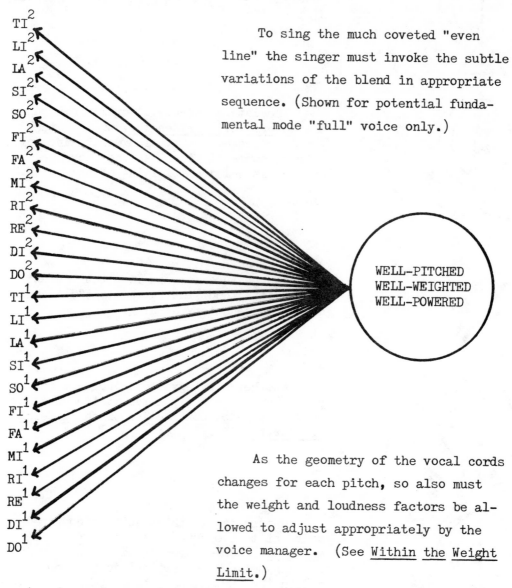

To sing the much coveted "even line" the singer must invoke the subtle variations of the blend in appropriate sequence. (Shown for potential fundamental mode "full" voice only.)

WELL-PITCHED
WELL-WEIGHTED
WELL-POWERED

As the geometry of the vocal cords changes for each pitch, so also must the weight and loudness factors be allowed to adjust appropriately by the voice manager. (See <u>Within the Weight Limit</u>.)

An advanced concept is born:

Pitch + Weight + Loudness = THE COMBINED LIMIT

The VIBRATO (see "Pulsation System") is the major indicator of
production within the combined limits of pitch, weight and loudness.
The vibrato provides a shock absorption system, inhibiting the onset
of vocal muscle fatigue. "When a muscle has been maintained in a
state of sustained contraction through repeated stimulation it grad-
ually loses it's ability to contract."

Edwin B. Steen and Ashley Montagu. Anatomy and Physiology, Volume
One. New York: Barnes & Noble, 1959, p. 95.

When the function is within the combined limits and the neural
pulso is unimpeded,   voice production can be free, both coordinated
and unforced. Sounds so produced will be characterized by:

Regularity   - The pulse will be regular
                      (periodic) through the range.

Quality   - Optimal basic (vocal cord)
                      quality will be produced
                      throughout the range.

Rate   - The number of pulses per
                      second will be appropriate.

Extent   - The amount of the pitch
                      change will be appropriate.

I believe it to be of considerable significance that the "Golden
Age of Voice", the Bel Canto, coincided with the acceptance (in
practice if not philosophy) of the concept of the pulsate voice.
Listen to historical vocal recordings for possible verification.

The VIBRATO (see "Pulsation System") is the major indicator of production without the combined limits of <u>pitch</u>, <u>weight</u> and <u>loudness</u>. The benefits of the shock absorption system are reduced by hyperactivity of the voice, the most probable cause of voice disorders.

Daniel R. Boone. <u>The Voice and Voice Therapy</u>. Englewood Cliffs, New Jersey: Prentice-Hall, Inc., 1977, P. 2.

When the function is without the combined limits the neural pulse is impeded, coordination is reduced and the free voice is replaced by a forced voice as the vocal cords are hypercompressed. Sounds so produced will be characterized by:

Irregularity	- The restrained pulse is an uneven, "wobbly" pulse.
Quality	- Basic quality is diminished to an owl-like purity.
Rate	- A retarded pulse has been described as a "tremolo."
Extent	- A widened pulse is another aspect of "tremolo".

These symptoms of vocal hyperfunction will diminish only as the excesses are reduced.

It was this vibrato, this major indicator of vocal excess, which was the object of the ridicule and scorn of those who defended the concept of the nonpulsate voice long after it's position was physiologically indefensible.

The nonpulsate or "straight-tone" production is function without
the shock absorbing, fatigue inhibiting vibrato.

Even within the combined limits of <u>pitch</u>, <u>loudness</u> and <u>weight</u>,
straight-tone sounds are characterized by:

Pitch — Reduced range, often one full and one falsetto register only.

Weight — Limited expressive range, particularly at the maximal end.

Loudness — Narrow dynamic range, especially at the maximal end.

Quality — Quality is retarded as the vertical phase system is restrained.

Flexibility — Diminished flexibility as the foundation of flexibility is the neural pulse.

Endurance — Early fatigue is predictable as repeated stimulation is unrelieved.

Longevity — The nonpulsate voice is a bad risk for a long-term guaranteed contract.

Without the limits, vocal hyperfunction without the neural safeguard
invokes a major sequence of penalties, ranging from dysfunction to
pathology of the vocal tissues.

Even today socalled musical purists persevere to achieve historical stylistic accuracy by utilizing a vocal style born of vocal
functional ignorance.

FUNCTION WITHOUT THE LIMIT

AN INSIDIOUS PROGRESSION: DYSFUNCTION TO PATHOLOGY

The penalty for extended function without the combined limit is dysfunction. (Add to function the prefix "dys-" and the definition changes from natural and proper to diseased, difficult, faulty, or bad.)

Dysfunctional voice is that vocal production which has become, as Thomas Conley, using the word in another context, termed it, DIS-eased, deprived of ease .... the laboring, forced voice.

Thomas H. Conley. The Healing Touch. Volume 1, No. 6. Atlanta, Georgia: Northside Drive Baptist Church, August 15, 1976.

As hyperactivity of voice becomes the norm and hypercompression of the vocal cords begins to take it's toll on the vocal tissues an insidious progression can and often does spin it's web of doom for the voice of the aspiring vocalist. Clear production gives way to breathiness, harshness, then hoarseness.

The beginning of the sequence, clarity, can ultimately be re-placed by a pathology of the vocal cords, sometimes in the form of a thickening of the tissues (hyperkeratosis) or in the more widely known hemorrhage within the cords (nodule), the dreaded vocal nodules or "singers' nodes."

We now leave the CLEAR, coordinated, easily produced voice to explore three phases of the insidious progression of voice dysfunction,

BREATHINESS, HARSHNESS, AND HOARSENESS

PATHOLOGY

Breathiness is literally the wind-sound of wasted breath which has passed between the incompletely approximated vocal cords without conversion into sound wave energy.

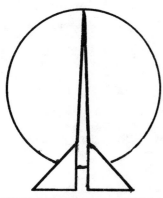

EXPRESSIVE BREATHINESS

Breathiness can be the result of elected hypocompression of the vocal cords. The vocalist chooses to leave the cords "ajar" for expressive reasons....the pain of the blues singer ....the rust of the jazz singer.... the passion of the torch singer. Or just because it seems expeditious to relieve the uncomfortable pressure on the vocal tissues. (See The Vocalist as Physiologist "Sub-minimal Compression")

NASAL BREATHINESS

Breathiness can be the result of air shunted through the nasal passages and out the nostrils by a vocalist who may not be aware of a condition such as a deviated septum which can interfere with palatal efficiency. (Note: Hypernasality occurs when sound waves are allowed to emerge through oral AND nasal passages. Nasal breathiness occurs when air, the breath, is shunted through the nasal passages in addition to or instead of the appropriate route of egress, the oral passage.)

OVEREXTENDED BREATHINESS

Too often, breathiness is the result of overextension of the combined limit (Review The Vocalist as Physiologist "The Over-Powered Voice"). When overextension breeds discoordination, postural compensation and hypercompression, the symptoms include:

- Loss of quality

- Slow, wide, irregular vibrato

- BREATHINESS

Continuation of the abuse encourages HARSH PRODUCTION.

HARSHNESS

The vocalist who disregards the "wind-song" with it's leaky alarm system and opts to continue overextension and attempt to turn off or at the least reduce the sound called breathiness can only succeed in creating a category of sound often called harshness. (Harshness con-

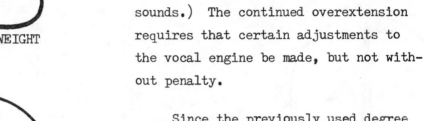

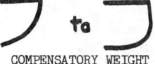

COMPENSATORY WEIGHT

notes disagreeable, grating, strident sounds.) The continued overextension requires that certain adjustments to the vocal engine be made, but not without penalty.

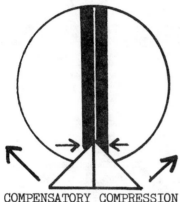

COMPENSATORY COMPRESSION

Since the previously used degree of vertical phase permitted leakage, the weight of the voice can be increased.

Side Effect. Reduction of quality and falsetto function.

Continued weight beyond the limit calls for increased compression and the usual postural modification.

Side Effect. Increased risk of tissue damage.

COMPENSATORY POSTURE

Additional weight and degree of compression require increased power (breath force).

Side Effect. Decrease of quiet dynamic range.

COMPENSATORY POWER

The voice can at this point in the insidious progression truly be termed a FORCED voice. Production is no longer easy, but requires an inordinate investment of energy. As fatigue increases and the ability of the vocal muscles to work cooperatively declines, the deadly progression gains impetus. Continuation of the abuse encourages HOARSE PRODUCTION.

If breathiness is a "wind-song" it is appropriate to describe
hoarseness as a "swan song." The modifications of harshness are as
a Band-Aid to a bullet wound.... ab-
surdly, pathetically insufficient for
the task.

Continued overextension of <u>weight</u>
and <u>loudness</u> with the resultant <u>hyper-</u>
<u>compression</u> creates the mutational
chink, leakage between the arytenoids
(glottis respiratoria). (Review <u>The</u>
<u>Vocalist</u> <u>as</u> <u>Voice</u> <u>Manager</u> "The Over-
powered Voice.") This is the ultimate
posture of FORCE.

DISCOORDINATION

The FORCED voice becomes a voice
of severely limited pitch range, eventually losing all falsetto production
and finally becoming a one-register
voice, often retreating to a subfundamental range as elasticity is lost.

At this stage of disorganization
the deterioration of the voice is evi-
dent. The <u>breathiness</u> remains as the
vocalist reduces weight and power as a
last-ditch defensive effort. This
subminimal compression brings ineffi-
cient modal controls so that the voice
is <u>unstable</u>, <u>noisy</u> and once again....
<u>breathy</u>.

REGISTER LOSS

Most disturbing of all is the
realization of the very real danger
that habitual misuse has created an
organic mutation. Continuation of the
abuse has encouraged

PATHOLOGY.

CAPITULATION

AN INDICATOR OF PATHOLOGY
PERSISTENT HOARSENESS

Temporary hoarseness caused by vocal excess can be reduced or eliminated by the cessation of the excess, however, if the hoarseness persists, there is reason not only for alarm, but for a laryngeal examination.

Abusive dysfunction can lead to organic dysfunction, a breakdown of the molecular structure of the vocal cords....pathology.

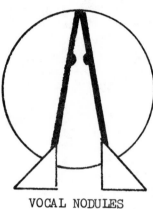

VOCAL NODULES

A well-publicized pathology is the vocal nodule or "singers' node." It is often born as a tiny hemorrhage, usually paired, at the junction of the anterior one-third with the posterior two-thirds of the vocal cords (as shown). With early detection voice rest can result in full recovery. With continued abuse the nodules become hardened (fibrotic) and must be surgically removed. The alternative for the unwise vocalist is the endurance of a relatively painless but serious impediment to effective and comfortable singing. (Pain is usually experienced as neighboring tissues are irritated by compensatory technique in response to the presence of the pathology.)

HYPERKERATOSIS

A common diagnosis is often described by the physician (to the patient) as a "thickening" of the cords. This callus-like pathology of the outer layer of the vocal tissues (sometimes "hyperkeratosis") can with early identification be corrected without surgury, otherwise, the cords can be stripped of the pathology.

Rest or surgury is meaningless without proper behavior modification. The rate of recidivism is high among professional singers who find it difficult to invest the time in a program of rehabiting vocal technique. The acquisition of and adoption of concepts of a Well-Limited Voice are critical to the well-being of a Credible Sing Machine.

WELL-LIMITED VOICE

Pitch   — Potential of three fundamental and two (prac-
                tical) secondary registers spanning two and
                one-half octaves.

Loudness   — Pianissimo to fortissimo.

Quality   — Complex package.

Flexibility — Florid ease in pulsate production.

Stamina   — Well-inhibited fatigue.

Longevity   — Candidate for lifetime warranty.

UN-LIMITED VOICE

Pitch   — Diminishing to one fundamental register plus
                a subfundamental and suprafundamental over-
                extension of a limited number of pitches.

Loudness   Reduction of quiet singing by degrees until
                only forced loudness at the forte levels
                remains.

Quality   — Owl hoots are fun....when produced by owls.
                Reduced quality plus sounds of the insidious
                progression of dysfunction.

Flexibility — Lessens as force increases and pulse changes.

Stamina   — Fatigue becomes the norm.

Longevity   — Uninsurable status.

THE CREDIBLE
SING MACHINE

THE CREDIBLE SING MACHINE

IN REVIEW

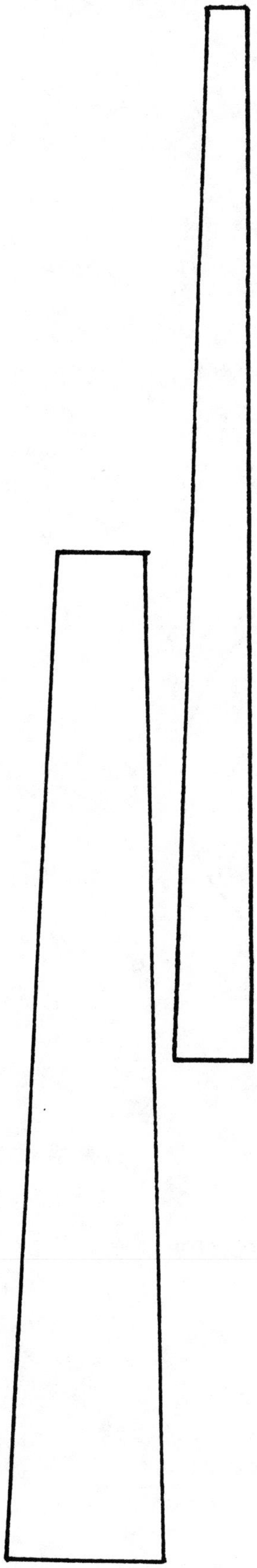

REGISTRATION

THE CREDIBLE
SING MACHINE

SECONDARY MODE PITCH RANGE AND REGISTER POTENTIAL

This Space Reserved For

ACOUSTICAL INFORMATION.

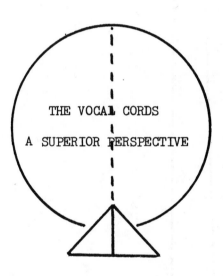

THE VOCAL CORDS

A SUPERIOR PERSPECTIVE

FUNDAMENTAL MODE PITCH RANGE AND REGISTER POTENTIAL

This Space Reserved For

PHYSIOLOGICAL INFORMATION

THE CREDIBLE
SING MACHINE

(SECONDARY MODE POTENTIAL)

(FUNDAMENTAL MODE POTENTIAL)

DO^1

All bodies have natural frequencies
of vibration. The basic frequency created by the full-length activation of the
body has been called a fundamental mode
of production.

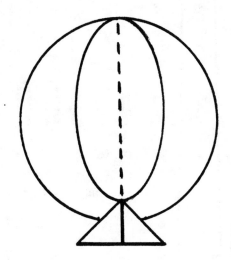

Every voice has a lowest terminal
pitch which is produced by the full-
length activation of the vocal cords in
minimal efficient tension.

THE FUNDAMENTAL PITCH OF THE VOICE

THE CREDIBLE
SING MACHINE

(SECONDARY MODE POTENTIAL)

(FUNDAMENTAL MODE POTENTIAL)

All bodies have natural frequencies of vibration. By altering one or more of the components of a vibrating body we create a new body with a different frequency. The resulting sequence of similarly produced frequencies has been called a _register_ in the nomenclature of musical instruments.

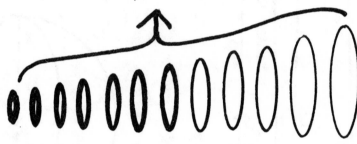

DO DI RE RI MI FA FI SO SI LA LI TI

As tension increases the vocal ligaments increase in length while decreasing in thickness.

TI^1

LI^1

LA^1

SI^1

SO^1

FI^1

FA^1

MI^1

RI^1

RE^1

DI^1

DO^1

ALPHA

The Alpha Register

As anterior tension is increased, the vocal ligaments are stretched, becoming less resistant to the air stream which powers the voice and thus raising the frequency. The span of pitches between DO^1 and TI^1 represents a register of fundamental mode pitches within the elastic limits of the vocal cords.

THE CREDIBLE
SING MACHINE

QUALITY
A COMPLEX PACKAGE

(SECONDARY MODE POTENTIAL)

(FUNDAMENTAL MODE POTENTIAL)

There are many natural modes of
vibration for a string, or an air column, or for any body at all. Vibrations
of strings and air columns in segmentation are quite ordinary even to the
casual acoustician. Quality is the
output of the combined package of modes
with their individual characteristics.

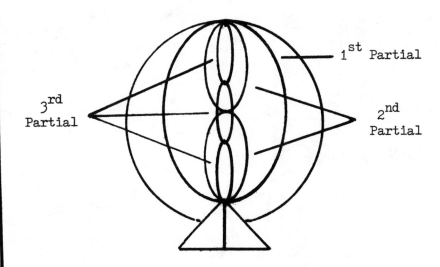

3rd
Partial

1st Partial

2nd
Partial

Alpha Register Quality

TI^1
LI^1
LA^1
SI^1
SO^1
FI^1
FA^1
MI^1
RI^1
RE^1
DI^1
DO^1

ALPHA

The pitches of the Alpha register
are heard as the fundamental frequency,
however, if the ligaments are able to
segment into halves and activate twice
for every one of the former, the result
is heard as increased quality. Increased
function makes possible as many as three
simultaneous modes of voice. The term
FULL voice is often used. (Additional
quality is produced in the air spaces
we call the resonation system.)

(SECONDARY MODE POTENTIAL)

(FUNDAMENTAL MODE POTENTIAL)

ti^2
li^2
la^2
si^2
so^2
fi^2
fa^2
mi^2
ri^2
re^2
di^2
do^2

ALPHA TWO

ALPHA (ONE)

"It is often far easier to set a body vibrating in one of it's overtone modes than in it's fundamental mode. It usually requires more energy to do the latter." Douglas Stanley perhaps unwit-

Clarence E. Bennett. Physics Without Mathematics. New York: Barnes & Noble, 1949, p. 78.

tingly defined the falsetto as an isolated secondary mode production by observing that the range potential of the falsetto corresponded to the "lower register tone" one octave lower.

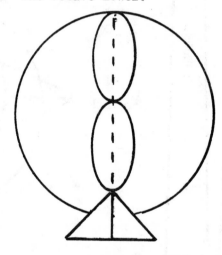

Douglas Stanley. The Science of Voice. New York: Carl Fischer, Fifth Edition, Revised and Enlarged, 1958, p. 322.

To produce the overtone without the fundamental the ligaments must be tilted to deactivate all but the thin edges of the cords while segmenting to achieve the socalled "falsetto." The range from DO^2 to TI^2 so produced is accomplished by the same tension changes used to create the Alpha (One) register.

THE CREDIBLE
SING MACHINE

THE BETA REGISTER
A SERIES OF FUNDAMENTAL PITCHES

All bodies have natural frequencies
of vibration. To create an additional
register of fundamental frequencies, we
must reduce the length of the string, or
column of air, or other vibrating body.
Because the geometry of the body has been
changed the additional effective range
will be less than that of Alpha (One) and
in conformance to the harmonic series.

(SECONDARY MODE POTENTIAL)

(FUNDAMENTAL MODE POTENTIAL)

ALPHA TWO

BETA

FI^2
FA^2
MI^2
RI^2
RE^2
DI^2
DO^2

ALPHA (ONE)

The Beta Register

The Beta register can be produced
by the stopping or deactivating of the
posterior half of the vocal ligaments.
Thus the resultant pitches are higher
and because the full length of the now
smaller instrument is activated they are
fundamental mode and are capable of
overtone production (as shown).

(POTENTIAL)

fi^3
fa^3
mi^3
ri^3
re^3
di^3
do^3

} BETA TWO

(FUNDAMENTAL
MODE
POTENTIAL)

ALPHA TWO

BETA (ONE)

ALPHA (ONE)

As the length of the vibrating body is reduced by segmentation the extensibility factor is reduced. Only the most supple of bodies can achieve the uppermost registers. This inability is reflected in the precise curtailment of upper registers in musical instruments.

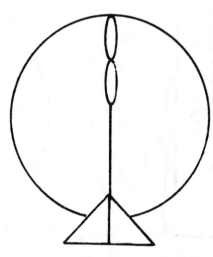

The Beta Two Register

To negotiate the Beta Two register the vocal ligaments must segment and the vertical phase relationship of the cords must be changed to the thin edge (as in Alpha Two). The posterior half of the vocal engine is deactivated (as in Beta).

THE CREDIBLE
SING MACHINE

THE OMEGA REGISTER
A SERIES OF FUNDAMENTAL MODE PITCHES

(POTENTIAL)

BETA TWO

OMEGA

ALPHA TWO

TI^2
LI^2
LA^2
SI^2
SO^2

BETA (ONE)

ALPHA (ONE)

Once again, as in the Alpha and
Beta (fundamental mode) registers the
extension of fundamental mode frequencies with the same vibrating body can
be accomplished only by further reduction of the active length. The further
geometric alteration causes the register to be of limited frequency span and
in conformance to the harmonic series.

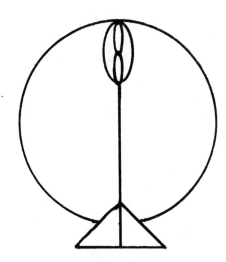

The Omega Register

The Omega register is achieved by
the reduction of the active ligaments
to the anterior one-third. The fixed
state at both terminals of the active
length provides for the production of
quality.

THE CREDIBLE
SING MACHINE

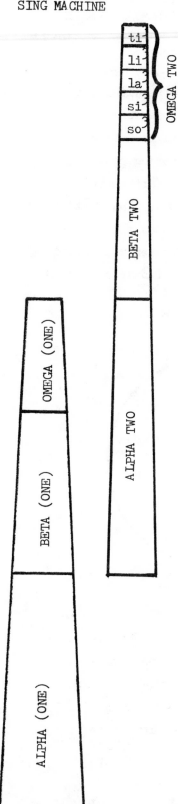

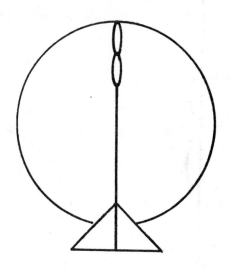

The rarest of registers, but who needs it? Only the most pliable vocal cords could negotiate this feat of segmentation.

The Omega Two Register

The Omega Two register is obtained by segmentation of the anterior third of the vocal cords plus the vertical phase shift to thin edge production. (Note: The Omega Two register is included only because it is theoretically produceable. It is both unnecessary and impractical.)

THE CREDIBLE
SING MACHINE

POTENTIAL PITCH REGISTRATION
AN ADEQUATE RANGE OF PITCHES

Realization of potential pitch registration provides a fundamental range of
DO^1 to TI^3 spanning two modes of production. Even without the rarely developed
Omega Two register, the remaining range
is more than sufficient for the requirements of voice literature.

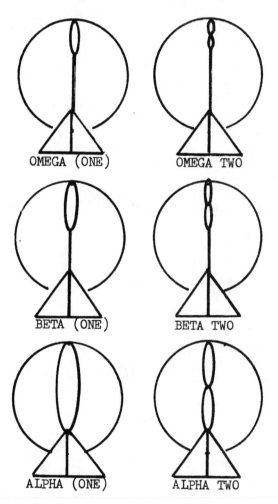

Potential pitch registration (sans
Omega Two) is possible only with regular
well-limited production. A critical
technique in the use of the potential
pitch registration involves the TRANSITION between registers and modes.

THE CREDIBLE
SING MACHINE

DO^1 THE FUNDAMENTAL PITCH OF THE VOICE
Lowest Terminal Pitch

$DO^1\text{-}TI^1$ THE ALPHA REGISTER
A Series of Fundamental Pitches

$DO^1\text{-}TI^1$ QUALITY
A Complex Package

$do^2\text{-}ti^2$ THE ALPHA TWO REGISTER
A Series of Secondary Pitches

$DO^2\text{-}FI^2$ THE BETA REGISTER
A Series of Fundamental Pitches

$do^3\text{-}fi^3$ THE BETA TWO REGISTER
A Series of Secondary Pitches

$SO^2\text{-}TI^2$ THE OMEGA REGISTER
A Series of Fundamental Pitches

$so^3\text{-}ti^3$ THE OMEGA TWO REGISTER
A Series of Secondary Pitches

$DO^1\text{-}ti^3$ POTENTIAL PITCH REGISTRATION
An Adequate Range of Pitches

THE CREDIBLE SING MACHINE
IN REVIEW

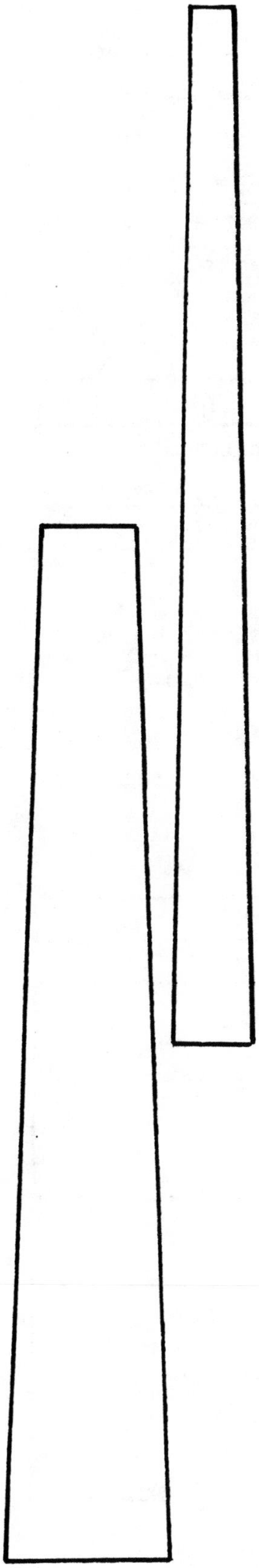

TRANSITION

THE CREDIBLE
SING MACHINE

LTP

UTP

LTP

UTP

LTP

UTP

LTP

UTP

The transition from one register
to another has been described in various ways. Such terms as breaks, lifts,
bridging the crack, the passagio, or
simply register change are familiar to
most vocalists. Points of transition
between registers of the Credible Sing
Machine will be termed "Shifts."

SECONDARY MODE SHIFTS

Each shift has two components, the
upper terminal pitch of the lower register and the lower terminal pitch of the
higher register.

The higher register always has the
shorter active vocal cord length.

Fundamental mode registers are mono-
segmental, while secondary mode registers
are bi-segmental.

FUNDAMENTAL MODE SHIFTS

Upper Terminal Pitches

Upper terminal pitches have in common maximal tension and minimal thickness
of the vocal cords.

Lower Terminal Pitches

Lower terminal pitches have in common minimal tension and maximal thickness
of the vocal cords.

THE CREDIBLE
SING MACHINE

THE FIRST SHIFT
TRANSITION FROM ALPHA TO BETA

The first shift often is unfamiliar
to the teacher of advanced singers, even
though the singer perhaps remembers earlier difficulty at that point of the
range. The transition becomes quite
strong (because of the midpoint reduction area) and equally unobtrusive with
time and well-limited singing.

The teacher of the child or adoles-
ent singer should be very much aware of
this shift, despite the fact that the
most common transition at that point is
between TI^1 in the fundamental mode
voice and do^2 in the secondary mode
voice (see "The First Switch").

Beta LTP - DO^2

The lower terminal pitch of Beta is
DO^2. The vocal cords are in minimal tension, maximal thickness, and half-length
activation.

TI^1 to DO^2
THE FIRST SHIFT

Alpha UTP - TI^1

The upper terminal pitch of Alpha
is TI^1. The vocal cords are in maximal
tension, minimal thickness, and full-
length activation.

Incredible as it may seem, most
singers have no second shift because
they lack the Omega register. This includes a number of professional vocalists who opt for a lower voice classification to compensate for limited
registration which translates into a
limited pitch range.

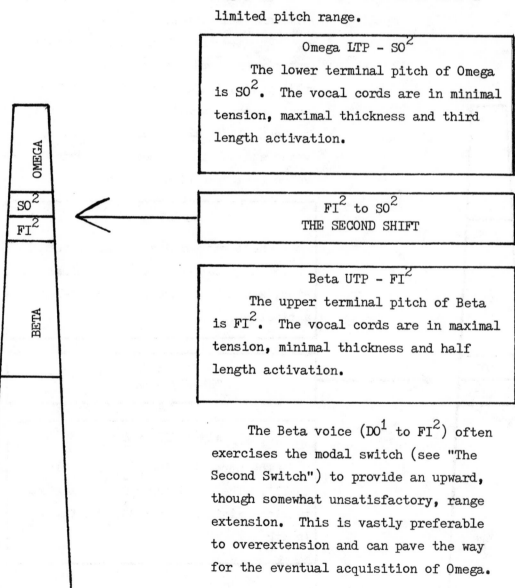

Omega LTP - SO^2

The lower terminal pitch of Omega
is SO^2. The vocal cords are in minimal
tension, maximal thickness and third
length activation.

FI^2 to SO^2
THE SECOND SHIFT

Beta UTP - FI^2

The upper terminal pitch of Beta
is FI^2. The vocal cords are in maximal
tension, minimal thickness and half
length activation.

The Beta voice (DO^1 to FI^2) often
exercises the modal switch (see "The
Second Switch") to provide an upward,
though somewhat unsatisfactory, range
extension. This is vastly preferable
to overextension and can pave the way
for the eventual acquisition of Omega.

THE CREDIBLE
SING MACHINE

THE FIRST SECONDARY SHIFT
TRANSITION FROM ALPHA TWO TO BETA TWO

The first secondary shift is in the realm of the falsettist. Not only the countertenor, but male and female pop singers employ this transition.

Beta Two LTP - do^3

The lower terminal pitch of Beta Two is do^3. The vocal cords are in minimal tension, maximal thin edge thickness and segmented half length activation.

---

ti^2 to do^3
THE FIRST SECONDARY SHIFT

Alpha Two UTP - ti^2

The upper terminal pitch of Alpha Two is ti^2. The vocal cords are in Maximal tension, minimal thin edge thickness and segmented full length activation.

After a Lily Pons performance it was reported that her effortless f^6 (the f above "high C") was accompanied by a look of surprise on her face as if she wondered at the source of such a high pitch.

This is typical of the response to Beta Two used as an upward extension of the pitch range. This technique is effective for light of weight voices because of the easy weightmatching capability , especially at high frequency pitches. It is usually entered via the modal switch (see "The Third Modal Switch").

OMEGA TWO

so^3

fi^3

BETA TWO

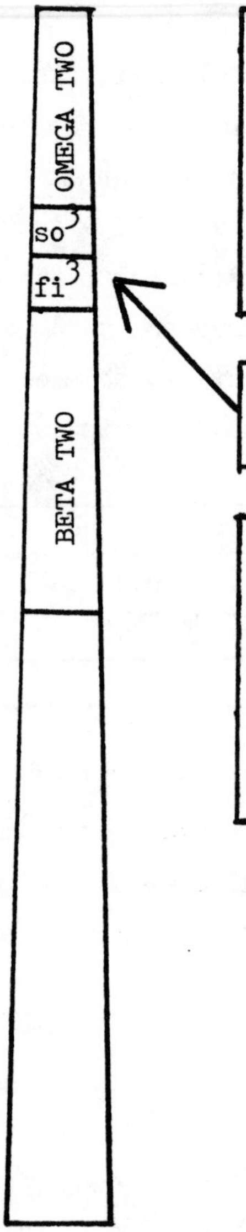

Omega Two LTP - so^3

The lower terminal pitch of Omega Two is so^3. The vocal cords are in minimal tension, maximal thin edge thickness and segmented third length activation.

fi^3 to so^3
THE SECOND SECONDARY SHIFT

Beta Two UTP - fi^3

The upper terminal pitch of Beta Two is fi^3. The vocal cords are in maximal tension, minimal thin edge thickness and segmented half length activation.

The second secondary mode shift is included here only because theoretically it is possible to produce Omega Two and therefore have a need for transition information. Practicality demands a reminder that the register (Omega Two) is physically impractical and further, that it is not required in the literature for the voice.

Information has been presented to facilitate the transition between all the potential registers of each mode. It remains to provide information concerning the transition between the modes.

THE CREDIBLE
SING MACHINE

INTERREGISTER TRANSITION
THE REGISTRATION SHIFT

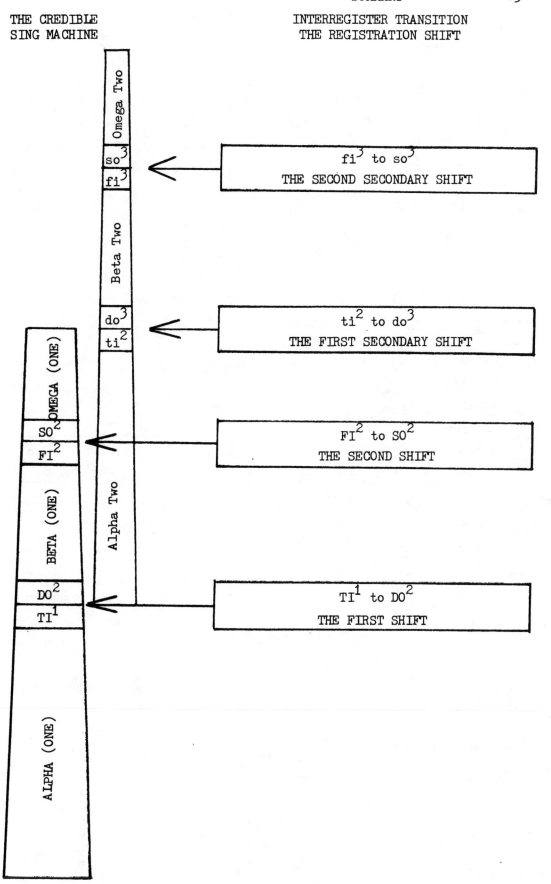

THE CREDIBLE
SING MACHINE

SECONDARY MODE

PARALLEL REGISTERS

FUNDAMENTAL MODE

MODAL SWITCHES
FOR EXPRESSIVE RANGE EXTENSION

MODAL SWITCHES
FOR PITCH RANGE EXTENSION

The fundamental mode voice, commonly called _full_ voice, is the major mode of voice. This is so because of it's superiority over the other mode in terms of quality, loudness and stamina....advantages of all mono-segmental modes over bi-segmental modes.

The secondary mode voice, commonly called _falsetto_ voice, although herein dubbed the minor mode of voice, can be used effectively as _an upper pitch range extension_ or as _an extension of the expressive range of the fundamental mode voice in parallel registers_.

In either use a SWITCH from one mode to the other is necessary. In the former, as many as three switches occur, depending on the extent of registration of the voice. For the latter, up to twelve switches can be accomplished between the parallel pitches of Beta and Omega in the fundamental mode and Alpha Two in the secondary.

THE CREDIBLE
SING MACHINE

THE FIRST SWITCH
ALPHA (ONE) TO ALPHA TWO

Objective: Upper Pitch Range Extension.

The first switch is crucial to the maintenance of the <u>child</u> <u>voice</u>. Habitual overextension, the alternative to appropriate switching, during childhood diminishes the coordination required to produce the Beta fundamental register.

The accelerated growth of the vocal tissues during mutation further contributes to the severity of <u>adolescent</u> <u>voice</u> problems.

Finally, the indescreet practice can result in an <u>adult</u> <u>voice</u> of severely

Alpha Two LTP - do^2
The lower terminal pitch of Alpha Two is do^2. The vocal cords are in minimal tension, thin edge maximal thickness and segmented activation.

TI^1 to do^2
THE FIRST SWITCH

Alpha (One) UTP - TI^1
The upper terminal pitch of Alpha is TI^1. The vocal cords are in maximal tension, minimal thickness and full length activation.

(POTENTIAL)

(POTENTIAL)

ALPHA TWO

do^2

TI^1

ALPHA (ONE)

limited registration which, because of it's one fundamental register will be called

THE ALPHA VOICE.

THE CREDIBLE
SING MACHINE

THE SECOND SWITCH
BETA (ONE) TO UPPER ALPHA TWO

(POTENTIAL)

BETA TWO

UPPER ALPHA TWO

so^2

FI^2

ALPHA TWO

(POTENTIAL)

FI^2

BETA (ONE)

ALPHA (ONE)

Objective: Upper Pitch Range Extension.

"What do you do Above your FI Two?" The choral soprano whose FI^2 is F-sharp^5 or lower has a problem. The G^5 represents over 4% of soprano singing time (according to a personal study). The temptation is great to overextend (or switch to alto). The penalty for overex-

Alpha Two Midpitch - so^2

A midrange pitch of Alpha Two is so^2. The vocal cords are in moderate tension, thin edge moderate thickness and segmented activation.

FI^2 to so^2
THE SECOND SWITCH

Beta (One) UTP - FI^2

The upper terminal pitch of Beta is FI^2. The vocal cords are in Maximal tension, minimal thickness and half length activation.

tension remains in _force_ (pun intended).

The appropriate use of the second switch, the alternative to overextension, can be a preliminary step to the acquisition of the Omega register.

Choral altos, tenors and basses have similar problems in meeting the demands of the choral literature.

The voice commanding two fundamental registers will be called

THE BETA VOICE.

THE CREDIBLE
SING MACHINE

THE THIRD SWITCH
OMEGA (ONE) TO BETA TWO

OMEGA TWO

BETA TWO

do^3

ALPHA TWO

TI^2

OMEGA (ONE)

BETA (ONE)

ALPHA (ONE)

Objective: Upper Pitch Range Extension.

The operatic coloratura literature calls for significant use of pitches a-

Beta Two LTP - do^3

The lower terminal pitch of Beta Two is do^3. The vocal cords are in minimal tension, thin edge maximal thickness and segmented half length activation.

TI^2 to do^3
THE THIRD SWITCH

Omega (One) UTP - TI^2

The upper terminal pitch of Omega is TI^2. The vocal cords are in maximal tension, minimal thickness and third length activation.

bove C^6 for the soprano. When the E-flat^6 of the "mad scene" (Donizetti: Lucia di Lammormoor) is well-sung it is because the third shift was employed as an upward range extension. Newspaper files are cluttered with accounts of missed E-flats or omitted ones (good judgment). When you consider that a Soprano in C-sharp can extend her range from a top of C^6 (TI^2) to G^6 (fi^3) by using Beta Two, her top (pun) priority should be the perfection of the third switch.

The voice having three fundamental registers will be called

THE OMEGA VOICE.

THE CREDIBLE
SING MACHINE

PARALLEL SWITCHING

OMEGA TWO

BETA TWO

TI^2	↔	ti^2
LI^2	↔	li^2
LA^2	↔	la^2
SI^2	↔	si^2
SO^2	↔	so^2
FI^2	↔	fi^2
FA^2	↔	fa^2
MI^2	↔	mi^2
RI^2	↔	ri^2
RE^2	↔	re^2
DI^2	↔	di^2
DO^2	↔	do^2

ALPHA (ONE)

Objective: A Wider Expressive Range in
Parallel or Bi-Modal Pitches.

Parallel switching has been taste-
fully and effectively used to widen the
expressive range by "serious" and pop-
ular singers alike.

I am reminded of the 1934 record-
ing of the "romantic" tenor, Frank Par-
ker (remember the tenor who for years
sang on the Arthur Godfrey radio program?), who finished the song "Two Ciga-

---

DO^2 to TI^2

The pitches DO^2 to TI^2 can be produced in either mode.

The range of expression can be increased by switching the Beta (One)
pitches to the parallel lower Alpha Two
pitches and the Omega (One) pitches to
the parallel upper Alpha Two pitches.

---

rettes in the Dark" (P. F. Webster and L.
Pollack) with a langorous full voice (fundamental) F-sharp[4] "in", followed by a
switch to a falsetto (secondary) F-sharp[4]
"the", then moving smoothly to the con-
cluding falsetto G[4] "dark." A stunning
performance!

Original Recordings of the 30's,
Volume 2, "Those Legendary Leading Men of
Stage, Screen and Radio." KH32430. New
York: Columbia Records, 1973.

INTERMODAL TRANSITION
THE MODAL SWITCH

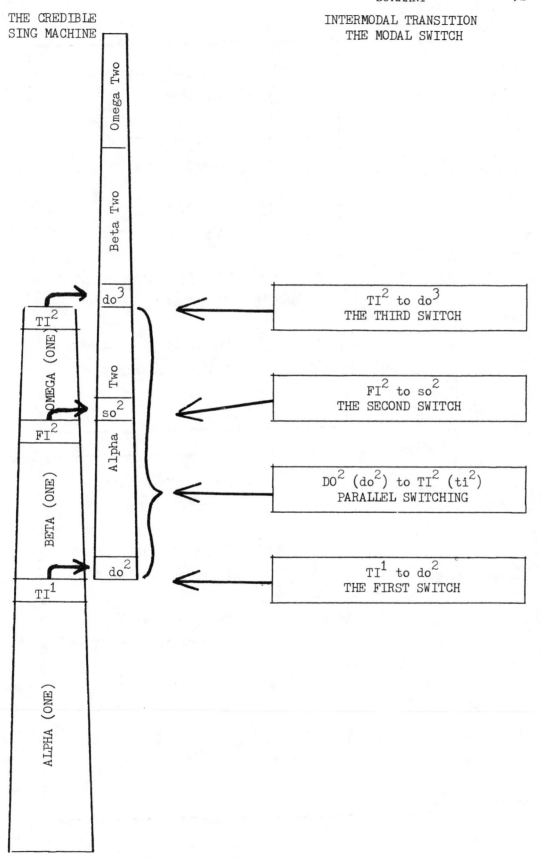

THE CREDIBLE
SING MACHINE

TI^2 to do^3
THE THIRD SWITCH

FI^2 to so^2
THE SECOND SWITCH

DO^2 (do^2) to TI^2 (ti^2)
PARALLEL SWITCHING

TI^1 to do^2
THE FIRST SWITCH

THE CREDIBLE
SING MACHINE

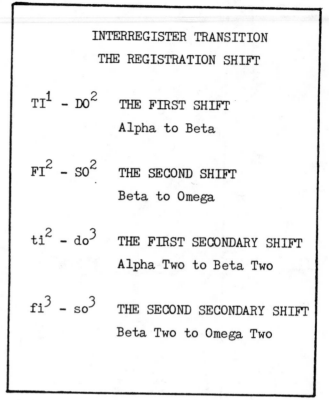

INTERREGISTER TRANSITION
THE REGISTRATION SHIFT

$TI^1 - DO^2$ THE FIRST SHIFT
Alpha to Beta

$FI^2 - SO^2$ THE SECOND SHIFT
Beta to Omega

$ti^2 - do^3$ THE FIRST SECONDARY SHIFT
Alpha Two to Beta Two

$fi^3 - so^3$ THE SECOND SECONDARY SHIFT
Beta Two to Omega Two

INTERMODAL TRANSITION
THE MODAL SWITCH

$TI^1 - do^2$ THE FIRST SWITCH
Alpha One to Alpha Two

$FI^2 - so^2$ THE SECOND SWITCH
Beta One to Upper Alpha Two

$TI^2 - do^3$ THE THIRD SWITCH
Omega One to Beta Two

$DO^2 - TI^2$ PARALLEL SWITCHING

THE CREDIBLE
SING MACHINE

THE CREDIBLE SING MACHINE
IN REVIEW

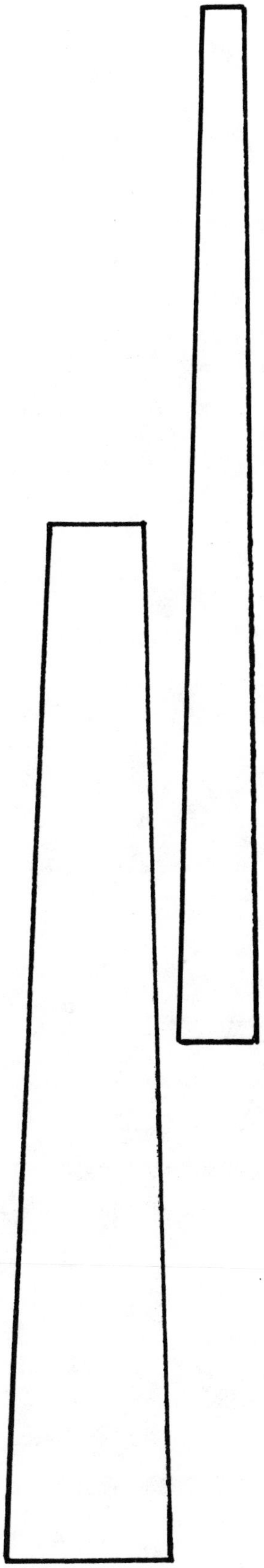

TESSITURA

TESSITURA

AN INCREDIBLE CONCEPT

The tessitura or easy range concept has been applied to both the music literature and the performing instrument. It indicates the general pitch range less the infrequent extreme high or low pitch.

Applying this definition, the choral soprano tessitura could be arbitrarily defined as the octave G^4 to G^5 because the soprano spends 86% of vocalization time on those pitches, this determined by a personal pitch distribution study.

Unfortunately for the soprano whose top singable pitch is G^5, within the tessitura, the literature study revealed that 1.04% is spent on $G\#^5$ and that a total of 2% is spent on pitches above the tessitura up to and including C^6.

Granted that all sopranos need not have those pitches above the tessitura, the fact remains that those high pitches are usually quite prominent as well as important to the literature in which it appears. All is well if the choral director elects to choose only that literature which is appropriate for his choral forces (no pun intended). I have observed that, voice range of the individual being a hazy area, many directors choose literature of excessive range and thus promote largescale voice overextension.

Tessitura in it's historical application has been cited here as incredible because of it's non-specific character which permits and to a large degree encourages the selection of literature which is unsuitable for voices with specific limits.

THE CREDIBLE
SING MACHINE

A CREDIBLE CONCEPT

Concept: If all pitches of the voice
range are produced within the
combined limits of pitch,
loudness and weight and have
the pulsate safeguard, it can
be said that the <u>well-limited
voice</u> <u>range</u> and the <u>voice tes-
situra</u> are one.

The onset of fatigue can at best be
delayed, for even the well-limited voice
has limits of stamina. It is well to consider the points at which fatigue will
first become a factor:

1. The higher the register; the
earlier the fatigue potential.
This is because the <u>reduction
system</u> places an additional physical burden on the voice.

2. All terminal pitches of registers invite early fatigue. This
is so because of the extreme
postural demands on the <u>pitch
regulation system</u>.

The importance of pitch distribution
in the literature brings a critical concept into focus:

VOICE TESSITURA
and
LITERATURE TESSITURA
Must Be
ONE

Concepts of tessitura will be reflected prominently in

HOW TO TRAIN
THE CREDIBLE SING MACHINE

Least Stamina

Less Stamina

Most (Secondary) Stamina

LEAST STAMINA

LESS STAMINA

MOST (FUNDAMENTAL) STAMINA

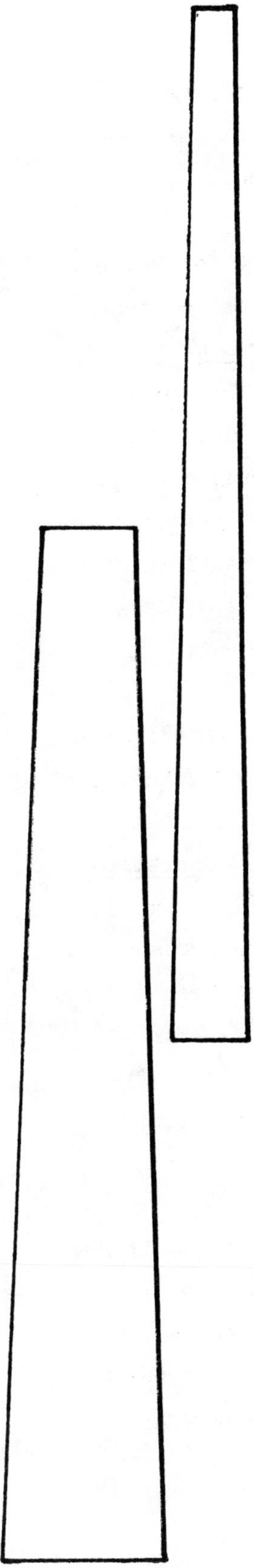

THE CREDIBLE
SING MACHINE

THOSE OTHER COMPONENTS

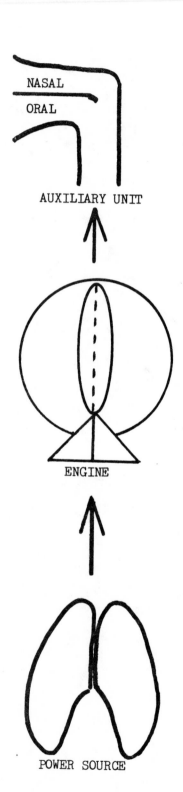

NASAL

ORAL

AUXILIARY UNIT

ENGINE

POWER SOURCE

"The Credible Sing Machine....How It Works" has been the story of the Engine of the Voice, the vocal cords.

It was not the intent to ignore or disregard that most critical component of any machine, the power source. It was rather that I find it incredible that we have attempted to deal with the power source of a human engine whose extent of function had not yet been defined. Having (to my own satisfaction) completed that task, I will offer a few words about breath management.

Nor was it my purpose to slight the remaining major component of voice, the auxiliary unit commonly called the resonator or it's subunit the articulator. I find it incredible to write about the refinement of the product of something which had not yet been defined in terms of it's physiology. For the same reason stated previously I offer a few words about resonance and articulation management.

A Credible Sing Machine requires the well-coordinated function of all it's components. The power source and the auxiliary unit of voice will be treated comprehensively in future works.

BREATH MANAGEMENT

Johan Sundberg took a casual position about breath management, stating that "....the vocal folds would vibrate no matter by what technique an excess of air pressure is built up below the glottis," but conceeding that "probably" some ways of breathing are more effective than others for singing.

Johan Sundberg. "The Acoustics of the Singing Voice" Scientific American, March 1977, p.23.

At the other end of the spectrum is a multitude of pedagogical authors who have focused their pedagogy on the breath to the exclusion of and often to the detriment of the vocal engine. This approach is akin to the selection of fuel for a vehicle whose power requirements are as yet unknown.

The truth lies somewhere between the two extreme positions. The concept which follows is a combination of those stated in the "Introduction to Vocal Physiology" (The Vocalist as Physiologist) and "Elastic and Muscular Limits" (The Vocalist as Voice Manager).

Concept: The power source, the lung system, fuels
          the engine, providing energy requirements
          for production of the full range of musi-
          cal expression within the combined limits
          of pitch, weight and loudness.

The breath, to be an effective power source for the vocal sing machine, must be partner with, not master of, the vocal engine. Without this supportive relationship neither component can long survive in a musical sense, and eventually the song is silenced....

Breath management will be treated in the depth appropriate for this major component of voice in

HOW TO TRAIN
THE
CREDIBLE SING MACHINE

A Few Words About the Auxiliary Unit....
RESONANCE MANAGEMENT

Voice production is the creation of one or more than one simultaneous partials produced by the vocal engine.

Voice resonance is the re-sounding or modification of the product of the vocal engine in the air spaces above the engine (see"concept")

Voice quality is the sum of the products of the two....the producer and the modifier. The quality should be even throughout the pitch range. The basic qualities of the voice are nasal resonance (the hum) and oral resonance (vowelization). Occasionally a combination of the two is appropriate; habitual mixture is unpalatable and is called hypernasality.

Voice articulation is accomplished by the modification of the boundaries of the oral resonance cavity.

> Concept: An auxiliary unit, the pharynges, the oral cavity, and the nasal cavity, tempers the output of the engine in it's role of resonator while the malleable walls of the oral cavity create the role of articulator, giving the voice the unique distinction of being the only linguistic musical instrument.

Inappropriate resonance can be the result of pathology, but can usually be classified as cosmetic dysfunction, correctable by posture modification.

The concept omits the long-time favorites of those who misinterpreted register changes as shifts of resonance to various inappropriate parts of the anatomy. I refer to the head and chest resonances which were labeled as incorrect nomenclature by Manuel Garcia before the turn of the century and proved to be insignificant at best by the acoustical and physiological communities. To those who label the sinuses as resonators or as voice engines, both concepts become unsound when the soft palate eliminates the nasal passages from the orally resonated voice.

Resonance management will be treated in

HOW TO TRAIN
THE CREDIBLE SING MACHINE

THE LAST PAGE

The Vocalist as Acoustician knows that all voices have a lowest
fundamental plus a series of other pitches produced by a pitch regulatory mechanism....because they have similar geometric characteristics,
will excite the harmonic series in similar sequence....because they
also have a similar manner of vibrational activation, will have similar registration....and being of dissimilar mass will have different
frequency range (pitch) potential.

The Vocalist as Physiologist knows that to produce the full potential range of musical expression the vocal cords must be....approx-
imated and separated....segmented (single and multiple)....latitudi-
nally thickened and thinned....longetudinally shortened and lengthened
....lineally stretched and recovered....laterally stretched and recovered....compressed and decompressed....and periodically lineally
loosened and recovered.

The Vocalist as Voice Manager knows that all voices must be produced within the combined elastic and muscular limits of pitch, weight
and loudness....that they must be protected by the pulsate system
called vibrato....that the penalty of un-limited singing is the activation of an insidious progression ranging from dysfunction to pathology....that well-limited singing is the only viable alternative.

This last page of How It Works is only the last page of the
beginning of a series. All subsequent works which deal with the "how
to sing" are based upon the concepts presented here as

                    THE CREDIBLE SING MACHINE

THE CREDIBLE SING MACHINE

Volume I

Part 2: Open for Inventory

Maurice L. Allison

To
John Maguire, Man of God,
Who helped me structure my Early Life,

And

Tom Conley, Man of God,
Whose example prompted me to Inventory my Later Life.

ACKNOWLEDGEMENTS

I celebrate all those Singers who, after Credible Inventory, embraced the concept of the Credible Sing Machine . . . and prospered because of it.

I thank my friend and colleague, C. Linden McIlvaine, Jr., Music Specialist, Prince George's County (Maryland) Public Schools, for taktime to render the invaluable service of reading the manuscript and communicating his Completely Credible Critique.

I am indebted to the vocal music students of Bladensburg Junior High School (1956-1970) who constituted the test group for the appropriate range concept of voice classification, the forerunner to the Credible Inventory concept.

I am grateful for the communication with many excellent vocal music teachers of the Prince George's County Public Schools (Maryland) who acquired in workshop (1974-1980) the then unfinished concepts of Credible Inventory and then applied them in the classroom.

PREFACE
THE CREDIBLE SING MACHINE
OPEN FOR INVENTORY

The preface to "The Credible Sing Machine....How It Works" described voice pedagogy as <u>incredible</u>....<u>unbelieveable</u>, stating:

> "Until someone can bring to vocal pedagogy a method which combines the sciences of acoustics and physiology and can present techniques which make possible the identification of the individual voice capacity and potential, we have no viable system of voice management...."

"How It Works" was written to clarify voice production in acoustical terms. Concepts of elastic and muscular limits were brought forward to establish the registration of the voice in terms of pitch, weight, and loudness. "How It Works" is the theory on which the series of works called "The Credible Sing Machine" is based.

Now the time has come for action....the "what to do." Now is the time for a new breed of vocalists who are also "acoustiphysiomanagers" (and you thought "supercalifr-etc" was good!) of voice to acquire techniques for the identification of the capacity, potential, and condition of the individual voice.

This inventory procedure is a preliminary to the introduction of a comprehensive program of <u>maintenance</u>, <u>development</u>, or <u>rehabituation</u> of the voice.

The Credible Sing Machine is now


```
OPEN FOR INVENTORY
```

INCREDIBLE VOICE CLASSIFICATION

"The Credible Sing Machine....How It Works" cited the inability of voice students and teachers to respond precisely to the request to "Describe your voice."

You are invited to participate in a brief voice exercise:

In five minutes or less . . . .

DESCRIBE YOUR VOICE.

1. Write the description.

2. Be as _precise_ as possible.

3. Be as _thorough_ as possible.

After you have completed the exercise (take more than the allotted time if necessary) turn to the next page and check your preciseness and thoroughness.

DESCRIBE YOUR VOICE
POSTTEST

Which of the following items did you include in your voice description?

Lowest vocable (possible) pitch .... ☐
Highest vocable (possible) pitch .... ☐
Lowest singable (easily produced) pitch .... ☐
Highest singable (easily produced) pitch .... ☐
Location of transition points ("breaks") .... ☐
Identification of registers by name .... ☐
Lowest falsetto pitch .... ☐
Highest falsetto pitch .... ☐
Location of falsetto transition points .... ☐
Identification of falsetto registers by name .... ☐
Category of function/dysfunction (clear, breathy...) .. ☐
Optimal voice weight (lyric, dramatic....) .... ☐
Description of vibrato .... ☐
Voice part designation (choral or vocal) .... ☐
Organic factors affecting voice .... ☐
Psychological factors affecting voice .... ☐
Chemicals which might affect voice .... ☐

Total Number of Items Checked
(For those who must) ☐

No, I refuse to give you a scale ranging from <u>credible</u> to <u>incredible</u>.

Traditional voice classification which has been based on range and/or quality is incredible simply because of it's nonspecificity.

Contents

THE VOICE INVENTORY

A preliminary to voice training is the gathering of data which has significance for the development and implementation of an individualized conditioning program. This "diagnostic-prescriptive" approach is based on the concepts introduced in volume one of the series, "The Credible Sing Machine....How It Works."

Traditional voice classification, which has been based on quality and/or range, must give way to a more comprehensive and less general procedure, the Voice Inventory. Inventory involves not only the specific listing of possessions, but the maintenance of the list by regular survey. This latter element has particular import for the growing voice.

A voice inventory is an instrument for the gathering of data which has significance for the development, or maintenance, or rehabituation of the voice. In addition to the increased specificity and more comprehensive character than has been traditional is the periodic assessment component of the inventory concept. To be an effective instrument, the voice inventory must provide the means for the acquisition of relevant information in an efficient manner.

An important outcome of the inventory process is realized when vocalists are able to monitor to a substantial degree their own voice maintenance. Since vocalists typically function as their own voice managers outside the studio, the awareness that permits vocalists to continuously monitor their voices in terms of the combined limits of pitch, weight and loudness is an invaluable asset.

Concepts for voice inventory will be introduced which are appropriate for voices at all developmental levels. While the actual procedures will be designed for the post-adolescent voice, some information will be given for application to the inventory of child and adolescent voices. (Child and adolescent voice inventory will be presented in depth in "The Credible Sing Machine....How It Grows.")

THE CREDIBLE SING MACHINE

PREINVENTORY

PRELIMINARY TO INVENTORY
A CHRONOLOGY OF SIGNIFICANT VOCAL EVENTS

The voice is today the sum total of it's original potential and it's subsequent use in all it's yesterdays. Many famous singers of the world, past and present, have been said to be the possessors of "natural" voices. A teacher must resent any implication that great voices are born and not made. I submit to you that one is born with vocal potential and can realize some portion of it, the amount determined by the appropriateness of the applied behaviour.

How then does the "habitual" voice begin? It begins with the imitation of human enviornmental sounds. The consciousness of the developing human is tapped by sounds which take on meaning and become prime models for the unconscious election of a personal mode of communication.

Before the advent of radio, phonograph, "talkies" and TV, the prime voice model was the mother, with the possible later usurpation of this honor by close relatives, friends of the family, and on occasion, the father. Recent generations have been besieged by a host of potential media models, among them the aging actor, who is loved long after the voice has become dysfunctive and unattractive; the heroic commentator, who has energetically reported tragedy to the nation while destroying his own voice in the expression of it; the rusty orphan, who sings of tomorrows and becomes a symbol of the young performers who will have no vocal tomorrows; and last, those legendary loves of our childhood, portrayed in a variety of vocal permutations, which give us the mice, ducks, and the whole "you-know-what" gang. Of course there are other, more appropriate, though perhaps less appealing models.

Outside the home environs, the church and school continue to exert a strong influence in the choice of the vocal expression of the young child. Dominating the scene has been that omnipresent societal attitude which insists that "big is beautiful" and that assertiveness begins in the mouth, so "let's all have powerful, deep, commanding voices."

We dare not move forward without a thoughtful backward look....

A VOICE CHRONOLOGY

A VOICE CHRONOLOGY

A Voice Chronology, or history, can be obtained by <u>interview</u>, by
the <u>completion</u> <u>of</u> <u>a</u> <u>questionaire</u>, or by <u>both</u>. It can be of narrow or
broad scope.

The chronology should include two critical areas of vocal history.
First, an annotated listing of significant vocal activity. Second, a
detailed listing of voice disorders. The two components can and perhaps should be combined, however, for the sake of clarity, they are
presented separately.

Chronology of Vocal Activity

The voice is now the sum total of it's original potential and the
effects of the use to which it has been put. The present condition of
the voice can be explained in large part by a review of it's past experience.

Chronology of Vocal Dysfunction

Most voice dysfunction is caused by misuse of the voice. A comprehensive history of voice disorders including all causes of dysfunction will provide essential information for the voice manager.

A summary of the chronology should appear in the diagnostic report
of the inventory and be made available to the physician should medical
evaluation be required prior or subsequent to the beginning of training.

THE CREDIBLE SING MACHINE PREINVENTORY
CHRONOLOGY OF VOCAL ACTIVITY

Name: First   Last

Date of Chronology

0 Birthdate [   ]   Birthplace [   ]

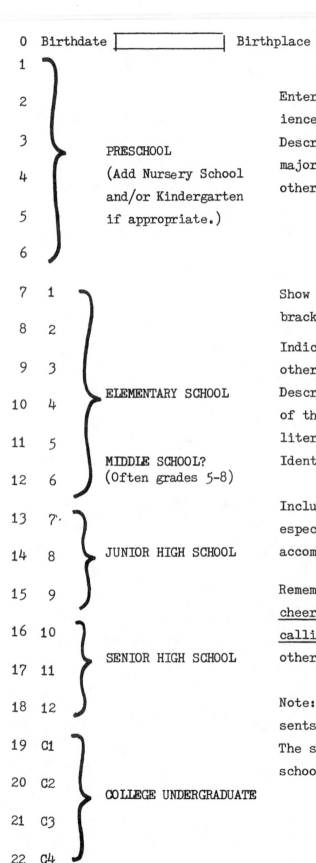

Enter early (preschool) voice experiences, including speech and singing.
Describe voice characteristics of
major voice models (mother, father,
other relatives, friends).

PRESCHOOL
(Add Nursery School
and/or Kindergarten
if appropriate.)

ELEMENTARY SCHOOL

MIDDLE SCHOOL?
(Often grades 5-8)

Show practical grouping scheme by use of
brackets (Elementary, Junior High, etc.)

Indicate school, church, community and
other significant voice experiences.
Describe musical organizations in terms
of their organization (SATB Chorus) and
literature (Oratorio, Cantata, Madrigal).
Identify the part you sang in each group.

JUNIOR HIGH SCHOOL

Include significient developmental events,
especially the mutation period and the
accompanying voice changes.

Remember to include activities such as,
cheerleading, quarterbacking, cadence-
calling for the ROTC Drill Team, and
other nonmusical, but vocal activities.

SENIOR HIGH SCHOOL

Note: The first column of numbers represents years of life ("1" = the first year).
The second column of numbers represents
school grade levels.

COLLEGE UNDERGRADUATE

1
2
3
4
5
6

7   1
8   2
9   3
10 4
11 5
12 6
13 7
14 8
15 9
16 10
17 11
18 12
19 C1
20 C2
21 C3
22 C4

THE CREDIBLE SING MACHINE PREINVENTORY

CHRONOLOGY OF VOCAL DYSFUNCTION

Name: First   Last

Date of Chronology

0 Birthdate [   ]   Birthplace [   ]

1

2

3

4

Enter by the appropriate year of life (column one) or the appropriate grade level (column two) events related to voice disorders. Use the following list as a guide only.

Symptoms of dysfunction.

5

6

Breathiness	Sore throat
Harshness	Dysphagia
Hoarseness	Other

7 1

8 2

Diagnosis of dysfunction. Give name, address and specialty of physician.

Laryngitis	Laryngeal polyps
Paralysis	Hyperkeratosis
Vocal Nodules	Other

9 3

10 4

Etiology (cause) of dysfunction.
Excessive vocal activity
Infections

11 5

Nasal	Laryngeal
Dental	Digestive
Pharyngeal	Other

Psychogenic factors
Other

12 6

13 7

14 8

Prescription for treatment.
Voice rest
Vocal exercises
Referral to Pathologist
Surgury
Other

15 9

16 10

17 11

Results of treatment.
Change of behaviour
Correction
Recidivism

18 12

19 C1

20 C2

21 C3

22 C4

THE CREDIBLE SING MACHINE

INVENTORY

	ti³ — Omega Two
	li³
	la³
	si³
	so³
	fi³
	fa³
	mi³ — Beta Two
	ri³
	re³
	di³
	do³
TI²	ti²
LI²	li²
LA²	la²
SI²	si²
SO² — OMEGA (ONE)	so² — Alpha Two
FI²	fi²
FA²	fa²
MI²	mi²
RI² — BETA (ONE)	ri²
RE²	re²
DI²	di²
DO²	do²
TI1	
LI¹	
LA¹	
SI¹	
SO¹ — ALPHA (ONE)	
FI¹	
FA¹	
MI¹	
RI¹	
RE¹	
DI¹	
DO¹	

"The Credible Sing Machine....How It Works" revealed that all voices have similar registration because of two commonalities (see "The Vocalist as Acoustician"),

1. Similar geometric characteristics, and
2. Similar manner of vibrational activation.

If that were the sum total of the statement the voice inventory process would be considerably simplified. All voices would have the same potential pitch range and the need for syllables "to dramatize parallel technique" would vanish. Pitch names would be appropriate for the similarly pitched voices. For the sake of reality, there is yet a third important characteristic of all voices.

3. All voices of dissimilar mass will have different pitch range potential.

To clarify this concept of similar registration based upon dissimilar pitch potential we return to Charles A. Woodbury's statement that

 "....so also is the human voice pitched to one or another key."

Charles A. Woodbury, Handbook for Choral Directors, Florida Southern College, Lakeland, Florida, 1951.

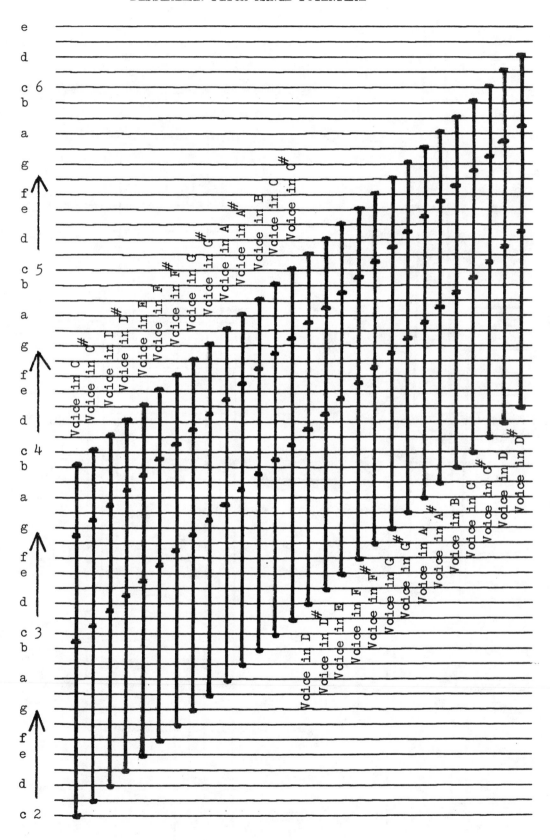

To clarify the dissimilar pitch range potential of the individual voice, we must return to the traditional (and very incomplete) vocal score.

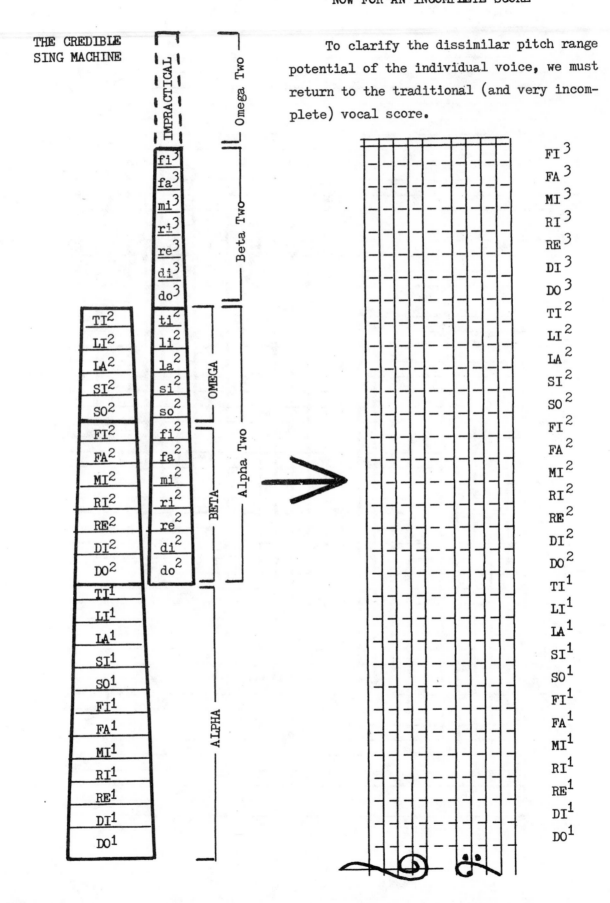

THE FUNDAMENTAL PITCH OF THE VOICE
REVISITED

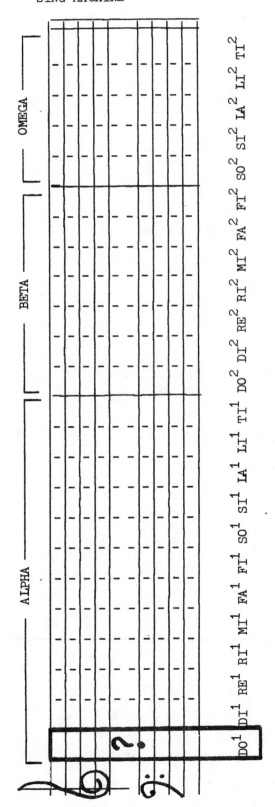

THE CREDIBLE
SING MACHINE

When I am asked to describe my voice, my answer begins with the somewhat comedic (to the uniniti- ated) statement, "I HAVE A VOICE IN E-FLAT^2."

Now, I have good reason to be- lieve that my true voice _frequency_ lies a few cycles per second higher than the stated key-note, yet sub- stantially lower than the next high- er traditional _pitch_, E^2. To insure practicality in the identification of the key-note of the individual voice, one must avoid preciseness which approaches absurdity.

Lest you forget, the fundamen- tal pitch of the voice, heretofore labeled DO^1, is the lowest pitch which can be produced within the combined elastic limit of the vocal engine, nee vocal cords.

It is not incredible to hear of voices pitched as low as C^2 or as high as E-flat^4. The models of society and the demands of the liter- ature make it less likely that you will hear many of these extremely pitched voices.

The identification of the fun- damental pitch of the voice is per- haps the major key (Hah!) to the realization of specificity in voice classification.

THE VOCALIST AS PHYSIOLOGIST

A HUMAN MACHINE

The voice is a mech-
anical unit of the human
body.

ENGINE

It has an engine,
the VOCAL CORDS, which
converts breath into
sound waves.

POWER SOURCE

It's power source,
the LUNG SYSTEM, fuels
the engine, providing
energy requirements for
phonation.

AUXILIARY UNIT

An auxiliary unit,
the PHARYNGES, the ORAL
CAVITY, and the NASAL
CAVITY, tempers the
output of the engine
in its role of RESON-
ATOR while the malle-
able walls of the oral
cavity create the role
of ARTICULATOR, giving
the voice the unique
distinction of being
the only linguistic
musical instrument.

The physiologist is concerned with
the function of voice. Once we have an
acoustically sound (no pun intended) concept of voice registration we can ask important questions. If the vocal cords
are indeed the engine of the voice, how
do they work? What is their function?

The scientific community affirms the
role of the vocal cords as the voice engine, citing the "breath passing between
the two vocal cords in the larynx that
vibrate to restrict and release the flow
of air" as the voice is produced.

McGraw-Hill Encyclopedia of Science
and Technology, 1971, p. 771.

The vocal cords ARE the engine.
They are composed of highly elastic ligaments, which, being elastic, can recover from distortion by force. The force
which adjusts the cords for a full range
of musical expression is muscular force.

The Vocalist as Physiologist will
explore the muscular movement and the
elastic recovery of the vocal cords, the

ENGINE OF THE VOICE.

PLEASE NOTE: THIS ERRATA SHEET REPLACES PAGES 13 & 14 IN PART 2.

INVENTORY ITEM I

THE FUNDAMENTAL PITCH OF THE VOICE

INVENTORY ITEM I
THE FUNDAMENTAL PITCH OF THE VOICE

A SKELETAL INDICATOR

The discernment of skeletal differences provides a general indicator of voice frequency (pitch) level, for a high corelation exists between the dimensions of the skeleton and those of the connective tissues of the skeleton, among which are the vocal ligaments (cords).

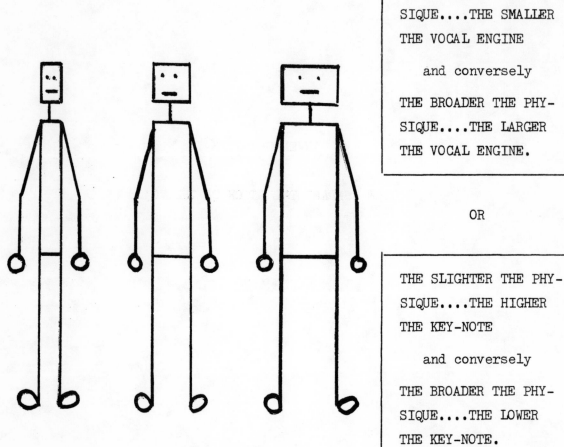

THE SLIGHTER THE PHY-
SIQUE....THE SMALLER
THE VOCAL ENGINE

   and conversely

THE BROADER THE PHY-
SIQUE....THE LARGER
THE VOCAL ENGINE.

OR

THE SLIGHTER THE PHY-
SIQUE....THE HIGHER
THE KEY-NOTE

   and conversely

THE BROADER THE PHY-
SIQUE....THE LOWER
THE KEY-NOTE.

Skills in morphological classification can be valuable to the teacher as an
instant general indicator of voice level.
There are variables to be reckoned with,
among them height, weight and muscular
development.

INVENTORY ITEM I

THE FUNDAMENTAL PITCH OF THE VOICE

A VISUAL INDICATOR

Concept: The Fundamental Pitch of the Voice is the lowest pitch
which can be produced without extraneous posture adjustment. (See "The Vocalist as Voice Manager.... A
Neural Deviation.... Downward Overextension.")

Once the <u>subfundamental</u> range is
entered, extraneous muscles which are
more appropriately engaged in the moving
of other parts of the upper skeleton
override the vocal muscles to lessen
vocal engine tension and create the "NO"
range....

TI^{no} LI^{no} LA^{no} SI^{no} SO^{no} etc. *

This indiscreet act is observable as a
turtle-like retraction of the jaw. This
manifestation of "un-limited" production
becomes a <u>visual indicator</u> of the lower
limit of the voice.

PROCEDURAL CONCEPT

Locate DO^1 by singing a descending
vocalization until an extraneous posture
adjustment is observed. Call the pitch
so produced TI^{no}. The fundamental pitch
of the voice is the pitch a half step
higher, the lowest pitch before the extraneous adjustment.

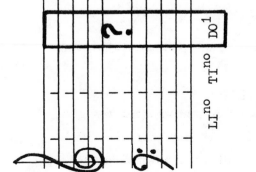

* See "Pitch Name Nomenclature," The Credible Sing Machine: How It Works, p. xvi.

INVENTORY ITEM I
THE FUNDAMENTAL PITCH OF THE VOICE
AN AURAL INDICATOR

Concept:

The Fundamental Pitch of the Voice is the lowest pitch which can be produced without tonal characteristic alteration. (See "An Insidious Progression.")

Once the subfundamental range is entered any of the following tonal permutations may be heard....

Reduced Quality. The vocal cords, with reduced segmentation, produce a simple falsetto-like first partial.

Breathiness. The hypo-tensed vocal cords are inefficiently closed and produce the sound of wasted breath.

Harshness. Over-weighted, over-powered, and hypercompressed vocal cords produce a forced sound, often called strident and harsh.

Hoarseness. The overtaxed, hypercompressed vocal cords combine the sounds of breathiness and harshness to create the sound of the noisy, hoarse voice.

PROCEDURAL CONCEPT

Locate DO^1 by singing a descending vocalization until a tonal characteristic alteration is heard. Call the pitch so produced TI^{no}. The fundamental pitch of the voice is the pitch a half step higher, the lowest before the tonal permutation.

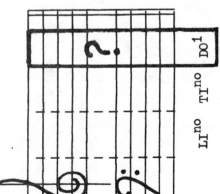

THE FUNDAMENTAL PITCH OF THE VOICE

A SENSATE INDICATOR

Concept: The Fundamental Pitch of the Voice is the lowest pitch
                  which can be produced without extraneous posture ad-
                  justment or tonal characteristic alteration.

Once the subfundamental range is
entered the singer must <u>sense</u>....

THE EXTRANEOUS POSTURE ADJUSTMENT
and
THE TONAL CHARACTERISTIC ALTERATION

Many of us are
fascinated by the art
of mimicry. The Mimic
knows which of the
voices is his or hers
because it is the
only one in his or
her repertoire which
is produced without
any superimposition.
The Vocal Mimic must
be keenly attuned to
the sensations which
accompany voice pro-
duction . . . . and
so must we.

A heightened awareness of the sensation of pressure (touch) which commun-
icates the internal postural adjustment,
and the sensations of sound which reveal
vocal cord function through interpreta-
tion of tonal characteristic alteration
is a requirement for self-inventory.

It is not enough to rely on others
for the perception of manifestations of
excess. It is essential that singers
monitor their own limits. Self-inventory
is a prerequisite to effective voice management.

PROCEDURAL CONCEPT

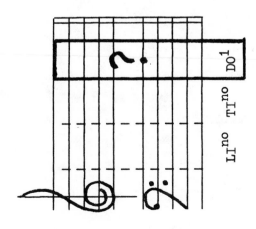

Locate DO^1 by singing a descending
vocalization until an extraneous posture
adjustment and/or a tonal characteristic
alteration are <u>sensed</u>. Call the pitch
so produced TI^{no}. The fundamental pitch
of the voice is the pitch a half step
higher, the lowest before the postural
and tonal deviation.

INVENTORY ITEM I
THE FUNDAMENTAL PITCH OF THE VOICE
A REGISTRATION INDICATOR

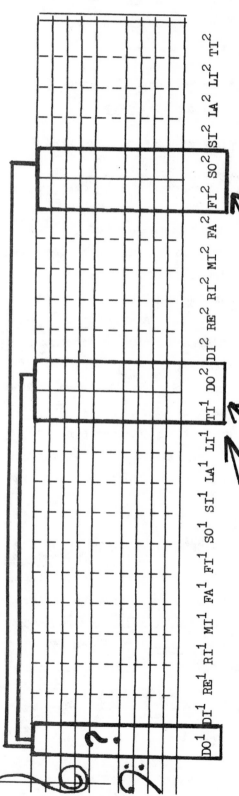

The most precise indicator to the Fundamental Pitch of the Voice is the relationship of this lower terminal pitch of the Alpha register to the lower terminal pitches of other fundamental mode registers, Beta and Omega. (See "Registration" and "Transition") Knowledge of the points of transition between registers makes possible an accurate prognostication of the Keynote of the voice, limited only by the inventory of limited registration voices.

The three-register <u>Omega Voice</u> will have a point of transition from FI^2 in the Beta register to SO^2, the lower terminal pitch of the Omega register. The Keynote will be the pitch a perfect twelvth below SO^2. (See "Second Shift")

The two-register <u>Beta Voice</u> will have a point of transition from TI^1 in the Alpha register to DO^2, the lower terminal pitch of the Beta register. The Keynote will be the pitch an octave below DO^2. (See "First Shift")

The one-register <u>Alpha Voice</u> has a point of transition from TI^1 in the Alpha "One" register to Do^2, the lower terminal pitch of the Alpha Two (falsetto) register, which can be used as an indicator. The Keynote will be the pitch one octave below Do^2. (See "First Switch")

THE FUNDAMENTAL PITCH OF THE VOICE

A SUMMARY OF INDICATORS

The teacher skilled in morphological classification begins voice inventory armed with a _general_ idea of the singer's voice pitch potential, based on a _skeletal_ indicator.

The teacher _watches_ for the extraneous reposturing of the jaw which indicates entry into the subfundamental range and is a _visual_ indicator to the Fundamental Pitch of the Voice.

The teacher _listens_ for the onset of tonal characteristic alterations which herald the entry into the subfundamental range and give _aural_ indication of the "Keynote of the Voice."

The singer acquires a heightened _awareness_ of the sensations of pressure and sound which reveal the entry into the subfundamental range and provide a _sensate_ indicator to the "Lowest Terminal Pitch of the Voice."

Finally, the teacher checks the results of all other indicators by comparing the intervallic relationships of the known points of transition between registers and the proffered pitch. This _registration_ indicator insures that the inventory has been a _precise_ one in the search for the elusive

FUNDAMENTAL PITCH OF THE VOICE.

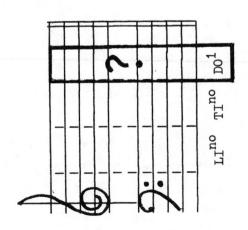

INVENTORY ITEM I
THE FUNDAMENTAL PITCH OF THE VOICE
SAMPLE VOICE IN c^3

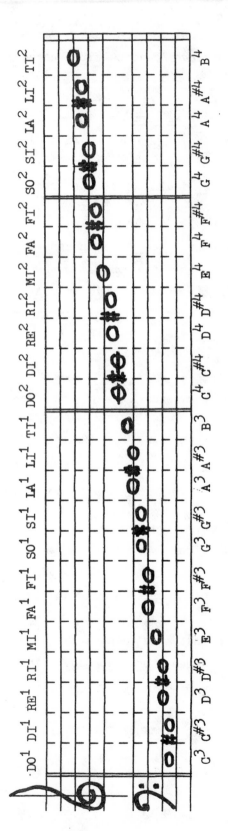

A voice inventory as a rule begins with a voice of unknown pitch range potential. To introduce the procedure for inventory, a sample voice will be revealed to you, the reader, with the hope that the advance knowledge will serve to clarify the techniques to be presented.

The <u>Voice in c^3</u> is a voice which is admirably suited to the tenor literature, lacking only that famous "money" pitch, the high C (c^5) in full voice. It is a very common voice, but was selected as the inventory sample voice simply because it fits rather well on the grand staff.

The subject (possessor of the voice to be inventoried) is of medium height and weight and of slight build.

VOICE IN c^3 PITCH POTENTIAL

Fundamental Mode (shown at left):
Lowest Terminal Pitch	c^3
First Shift	$B^3 - c^4$
Second Shift	$F^{\#4} - G^4$
Highest Terminal Pitch	B^4

Secondary Mode (not shown):
Lowest Terminal Pitch	c^4
First Shift	$b^4 - c^5$
Second Shift (impractical)	
Highest Terminal Pitch	$f^{\#5}$

INVENTORY ITEM I
THE FUNDAMENTAL PITCH OF THE VOICE
INVENTORY VOCALIZATION

Procedural Concept: Locate DO^1 by singing a descending vocalization until the entry to the subfundamental range is seen, heard or sensed. Call the pitch so produced TI^{no}. Count upward one half step to DO^1, the Fundamental Pitch of the Voice.

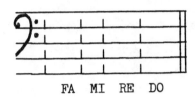

FA MI RE DO

The inventory vocalization should be of narrow enough range to permit a number of descending statements before the terminal pitch area is reached. I have selected the progression

          FA

                  MI

                          RE

                                  DO.

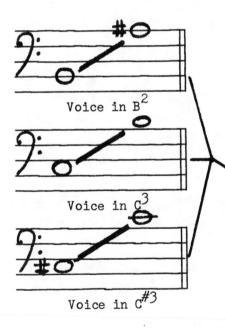

Voice in B^2

Voice in C^3

Voice in $C^{\#3}$

The appropriate pitch level for the start of the inventory can be estimated by the utilization of the skeletal indicator. The subject is approximately 5' 10" tall and weighs about 155 pounds on a slight frame.

The "guesstimate" based on the above is that the subject's voice is in B^2, C^3, or $C^{\#3}$.

The inventory vocalization should be confined to the pitch limits of the Alpha register. It should begin no higher than TI^1 of the lowest voice listed (B) and end no lower than MI^1 of the highest listed voice ($C^{\#}$). I have selected as the pitch level for the start of the inventory vocalization B^{b3}.

B^b A G F

INVENTORY ITEM I
THE FUNDAMENTAL PITCH OF THE VOICE
PRELIMINARY INSTRUCTIONS

TO THE SUBJECT

1. "Stand facing there so I can observe you in profile while you sing."

   — — — — — — — — —

2. "Do not change your posture because of the microphone. Be concerned with using whatever posture you ordinarily use while singing."

   — — — — — — — — —

3. "I will sit at the keyboard to give any necessary pitches. I will not use my singing voice during inventory because of the possibility that it could affect your performance."

   — — — — — — — — —

4. "Posture is very important to good singing. Begin with your best posture for singing and do not change it, no matter what pitch you must sing."

   — — — — — — — — —

5. "When you are asked to sing a pitch which is so low that you feel the need to adjust your posture in some way, stop immediately afterward and tell me."

   — — — — — — — — —

6. "Sing the vocalizations as smoothly as possible....maintaining a slow tempo.... with moderate loudness.... on the vowel 'AH'. Or would you prefer another vowel?"

TO THE READER

Profile observation (side view) facilitates detection of postural modification.

— — — — — — — — —

The session is taped for the gathering of additional data. Nothing must interfere with the subject's habitual vocal practices. (Consider vidiotape.)

— — — — — — — — —

The subject must be inventoried without the distraction of a perhaps incorrect model. My voice in E^{b2} could disorient the subject in terms of pitch, weight or pulse characteristics.

— — — — — — — — —

The first vocalizations should be easily produced. At no time will the subject be permitted to adjust his posture to expedite the singing of lower pitches.

— — — — — — — — —

While the subject is bringing the sensate indicator into play, the inventoryer employs the visual and aural indicators to identify TI^{no} and subsequently locate the Fundamental Pitch of the Voice.

— — — — — — — — —

LEGATO

LENTO

MEZZO PIANO

MONO-VOWELIC

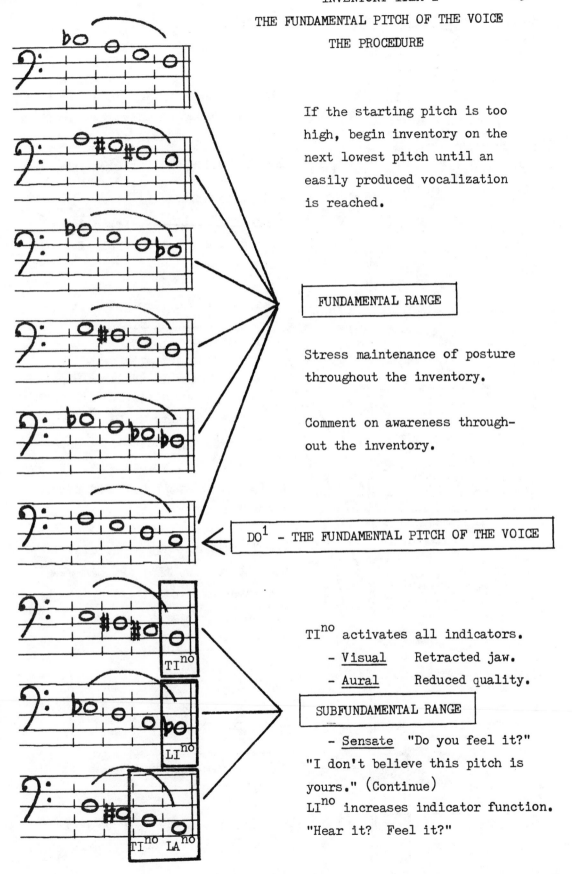

If the starting pitch is too
high, begin inventory on the
next lowest pitch until an
easily produced vocalization
is reached.

FUNDAMENTAL RANGE

Stress maintenance of posture
throughout the inventory.

Comment on awareness throughout the inventory.

DO^1 - THE FUNDAMENTAL PITCH OF THE VOICE

TI^{no} activates all indicators.
- Visual   Retracted jaw.
- Aural   Reduced quality.

SUBFUNDAMENTAL RANGE

- Sensate "Do you feel it?"
"I don't believe this pitch is
yours." (Continue)
LI^{no} increases indicator function.
"Hear it? Feel it?"

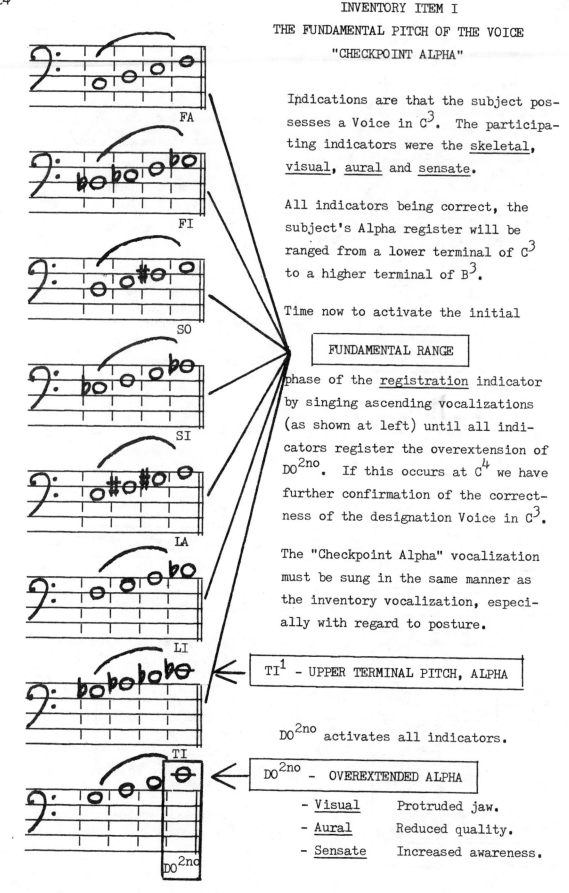

INVENTORY ITEM I

THE FUNDAMENTAL PITCH OF THE VOICE

"CHECKPOINT ALPHA"

Indications are that the subject possesses a Voice in c^3. The participating indicators were the skeletal, visual, aural and sensate.

All indicators being correct, the subject's Alpha register will be ranged from a lower terminal of c^3 to a higher terminal of B^3.

Time now to activate the initial

FUNDAMENTAL RANGE

phase of the registration indicator by singing ascending vocalizations (as shown at left) until all indicators register the overextension of DO^{2no}. If this occurs at c^4 we have further confirmation of the correctness of the designation Voice in c^3.

The "Checkpoint Alpha" vocalization must be sung in the same manner as the inventory vocalization, especially with regard to posture.

TI^1 - UPPER TERMINAL PITCH, ALPHA

DO^{2no} activates all indicators.

DO^{2no} - OVEREXTENDED ALPHA

- Visual   Protruded jaw.
- Aural   Reduced quality.
- Sensate   Increased awareness.

THE FUNDAMENTAL PITCH OF THE VOICE
ACTUAL AND POTENTIAL

POTENTIAL RANGE

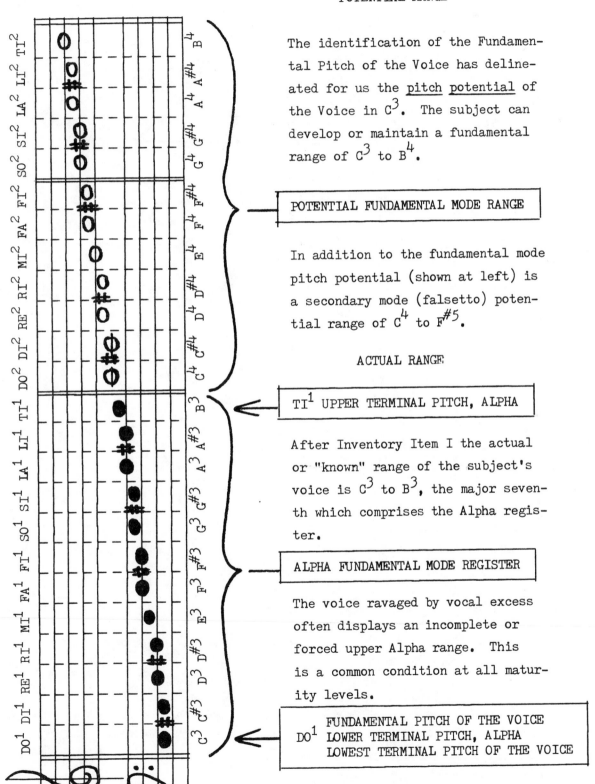

The identification of the Fundamental Pitch of the Voice has delineated for us the <u>pitch</u> <u>potential</u> of the Voice in C^3. The subject can develop or maintain a fundamental range of C^3 to B^4.

| POTENTIAL FUNDAMENTAL MODE RANGE |

In addition to the fundamental mode pitch potential (shown at left) is a secondary mode (falsetto) potential range of C^4 to $F^{\#5}$.

ACTUAL RANGE

| TI^1 UPPER TERMINAL PITCH, ALPHA |

After Inventory Item I the actual or "known" range of the subject's voice is C^3 to B^3, the major seventh which comprises the Alpha register.

| ALPHA FUNDAMENTAL MODE REGISTER |

The voice ravaged by vocal excess often displays an incomplete or forced upper Alpha range. This is a common condition at all maturity levels.

| DO^1 FUNDAMENTAL PITCH OF THE VOICE LOWER TERMINAL PITCH, ALPHA LOWEST TERMINAL PITCH OF THE VOICE |

INVENTORY ITEM II

EXTENT OF REGISTRATION

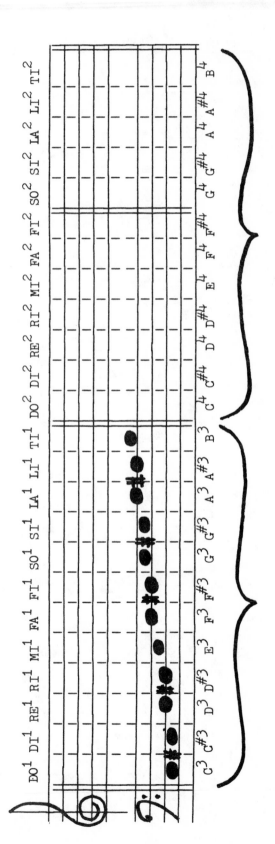

Thus far we know the subject to
have an Alpha register which ranges
from C^3 to B^3 (DO^1 to TI^1).

Inventory Item II is designed to
reveal the extent of registration
of this Voice in C^3. What happens
above the known B^3?

UNKNOWN

The potential registration of the
Voice in C^3 is known. It's present
stage of development is unknown.

Inventory Item II will be accomplished through the singing of three
(or less) vocalizations which will
by the identification of the actual*
be prerequisite to the assignment
of a plan of action for the development of the potential.*

KNOWN

But first, give close attention to
some critical phases of development
of the Credible Sing Machine.

* Actual or Potential pitch range.

EXTENT OF REGISTRATION

PHASES OF REGISTRATION DEVELOPMENT

ORGANIZATION OF INFORMATION

PITCH EXTENT: (Registers in parentheses)

$\left(\dfrac{\text{FUNDAMENTAL REGISTERS in upper case}}{\text{Secondary Registers in lower case}}\right)$

+ Indicates the use of secondary register to aug-
  ment range.

THIS SPACE RESERVED FOR

ADDITIONAL INFORMATION.

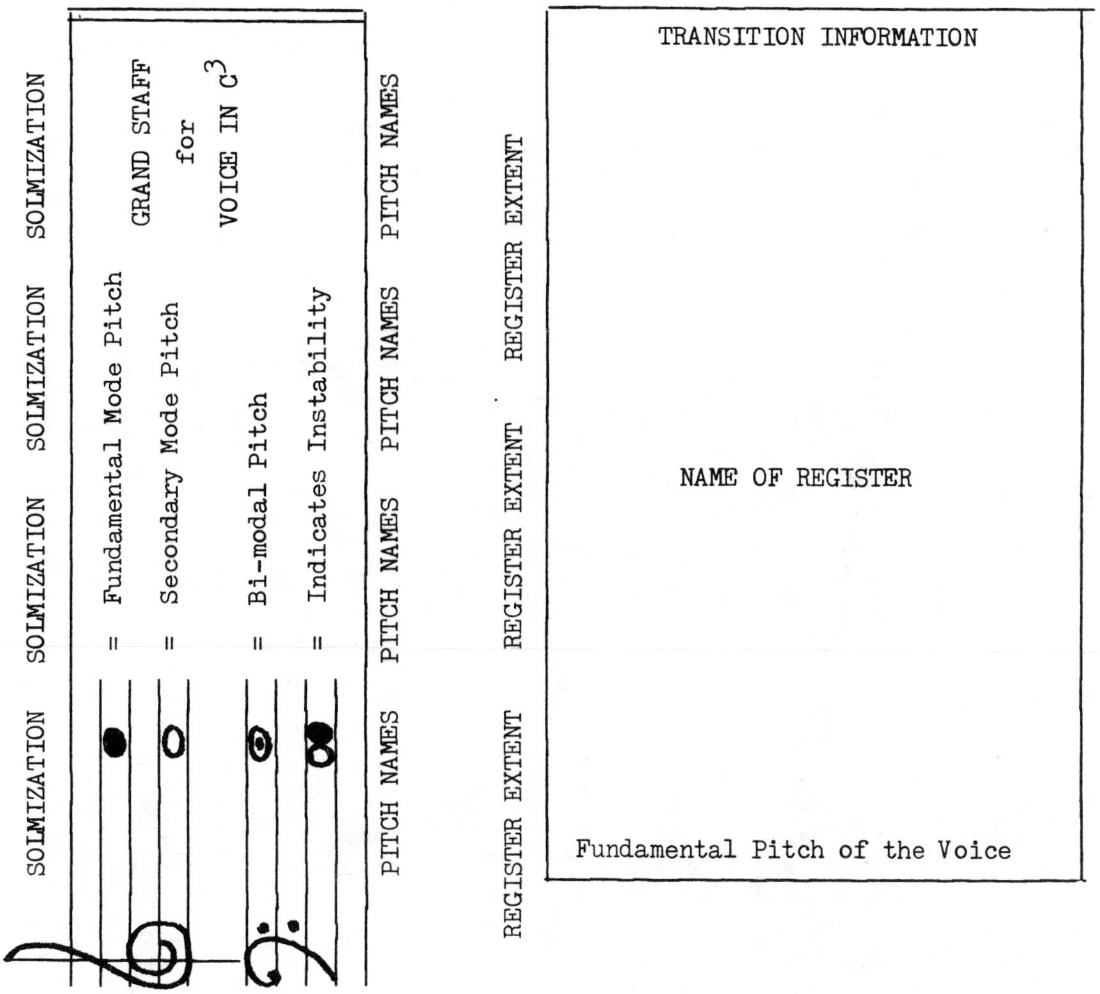

POTENTIAL RANGE

SOLMIZATION SOLMIZATION SOLMIZATION SOLMIZATION

= Fundamental Mode Pitch

= Secondary Mode Pitch

= Bi-modal Pitch

= Indicates Instability

GRAND STAFF

for

VOICE IN c^3

PITCH NAMES PITCH NAMES PITCH NAMES

PITCH NAMES

REGISTER EXTENT REGISTER EXTENT

REGISTER EXTENT

TRANSITION INFORMATION

NAME OF REGISTER

Fundamental Pitch of the Voice

Pitch Extent: (DO^1 to less than TI^1)

The incomplete Alpha voice is often the result of un-limited singing in terms of <u>pitch</u>, <u>loudness</u> or <u>weight</u>.

Sometimes the Alpha Minus voice can be produced in the secondary mode Alpha Two register, duplicating the range shown (at left) one octave higher. It is more likely that hyperfunction of the voice has resulted in a mono-modal voice, possibly only a temporary condition.

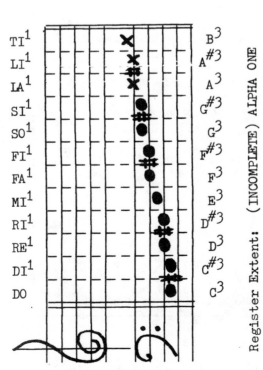

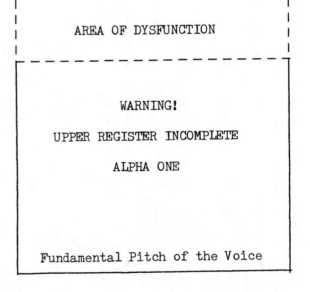

AREA OF DYSFUNCTION

WARNING!

UPPER REGISTER INCOMPLETE

ALPHA ONE

Fundamental Pitch of the Voice

Pitch Extent: (DO^1 to TI^1)

The single mode Alpha voice is the
result of hypercompression of the
vocal cords, a condition created by
hyperfunction of the voice.

The secondary mode Alpha Two register cannot be produced, as the thin-
edge posture cannot be assumed by
the cords until the compression is
moderated.

POTENTIAL POTENTIAL

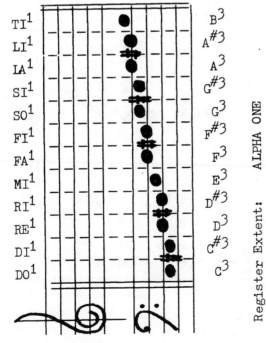

Register Extent: ALPHA ONE

DEAD END!

ALPHA ONE

Fundamental Pitch of the Voice

Pitch Extent: $(DO^1$ to $TI^1)$ $(\dfrac{- - -}{do^2 \text{ to } ti^2})$

The Alpha Plus voice is the total Alpha voice. The discipline to switch to the secondary mode as an alternative to overextension is a prerequisite to the development of the Beta voice.

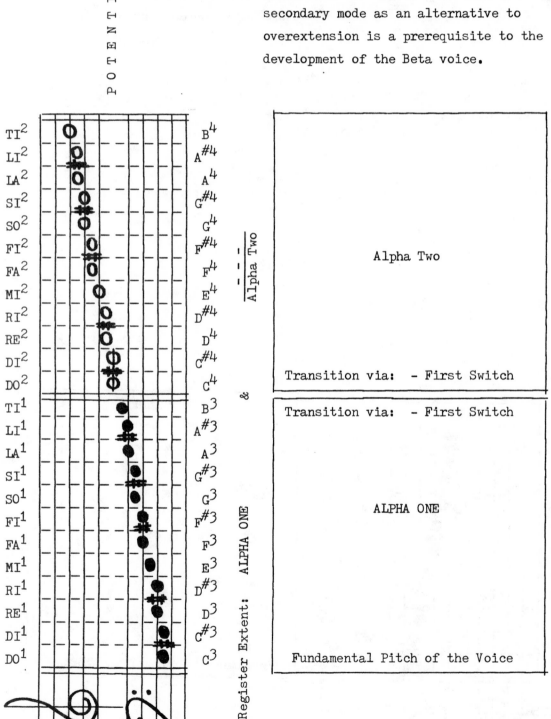

Alpha Two	
Transition via:	– First Switch
Transition via:	– First Switch
ALPHA ONE	
Fundamental Pitch of the Voice	

Pitch Extent: (DO^1 to TI^1) ($\frac{\text{Sometimes } DO^2 \text{ to } FI^2}{\text{Sometimes } do^2 \text{ to } fi^2}$)

Disconcerting to the new Beta vocalist is the temporary instability of the register. For a time, the modal controls can be unreliable and unpredictable, fluctuating between the fundamental mode Beta One and the parallel secondary mode Alpha Two. (Note: Upper Alpha Two is omitted here because of it's relative unimportance to the "Beta Minus" phase.

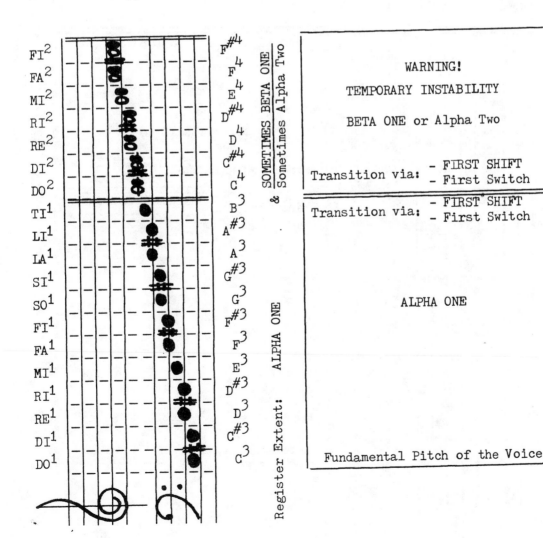

WARNING!

TEMPORARY INSTABILITY

BETA ONE or Alpha Two

Transition via: - FIRST SHIFT
                 - First Switch

Transition via: - FIRST SHIFT
                 - First Switch

ALPHA ONE

Fundamental Pitch of the Voice

Pitch Extent: $\quad (DO^1 \text{ to } TI^1) \ \left(\dfrac{DO^2 \text{ to } FI^2}{do^2 \text{ to } fi^2}\right) + \left(\dfrac{- - -}{so^2 \text{ to } ti^2}\right)$

The established Beta vocalist will, as a preliminary to the development of the Omega voice, extend the upper range by the temporary use of the upper Alpha Two range. This is an important alternative to range overextension.

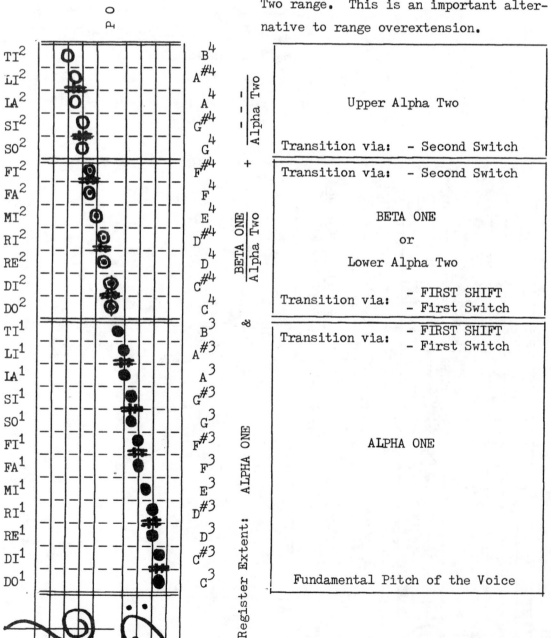

Upper Alpha Two	
Transition via:	- Second Switch
Transition via:	- Second Switch
BETA ONE or Lower Alpha Two	
Transition via:	- FIRST SHIFT - First Switch
Transition via:	- FIRST SHIFT - First Switch
ALPHA ONE	
Fundamental Pitch of the Voice	

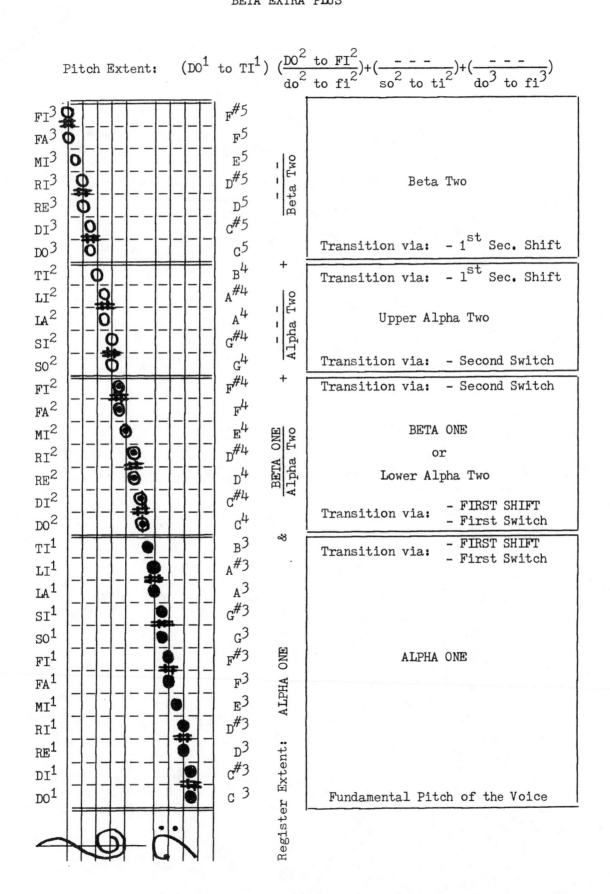

Pitch Extent: $(DO^1$ to $TI^1)$ $(\dfrac{DO^2 \text{ to } FI^2}{do^2 \text{ to } fi^2})$$+(\dfrac{- - -}{so^2 \text{ to } ti^2})$$+(\dfrac{- - -}{do^3 \text{ to } fi^3})$

Beta Two

Transition via: - 1st Sec. Shift

Transition via: - 1st Sec. Shift

Upper Alpha Two

Transition via: - Second Switch

Transition via: - Second Switch

BETA ONE

or

Lower Alpha Two

Transition via: - FIRST SHIFT
                 - First Switch

Transition via: - FIRST SHIFT
                 - First Switch

ALPHA ONE

Fundamental Pitch of the Voice

Pitch Extent: $(DO^1$ to $TI^1)$ $\left(\dfrac{DO^2 \text{ to } FI^2}{do^2 \text{ to } fi^2}\right)$ $\left(\dfrac{\text{SOMETIMES } SO^2 \text{ to } TI^2}{\text{Sometimes } so^2 \text{ to } ti^2}\right)$

Like the early Beta voice, the new Omega voice is characterized by an uncertain fundamental Omega register, which sometimes switches without warning to the parallel secondary (upper) Alpha Two register.

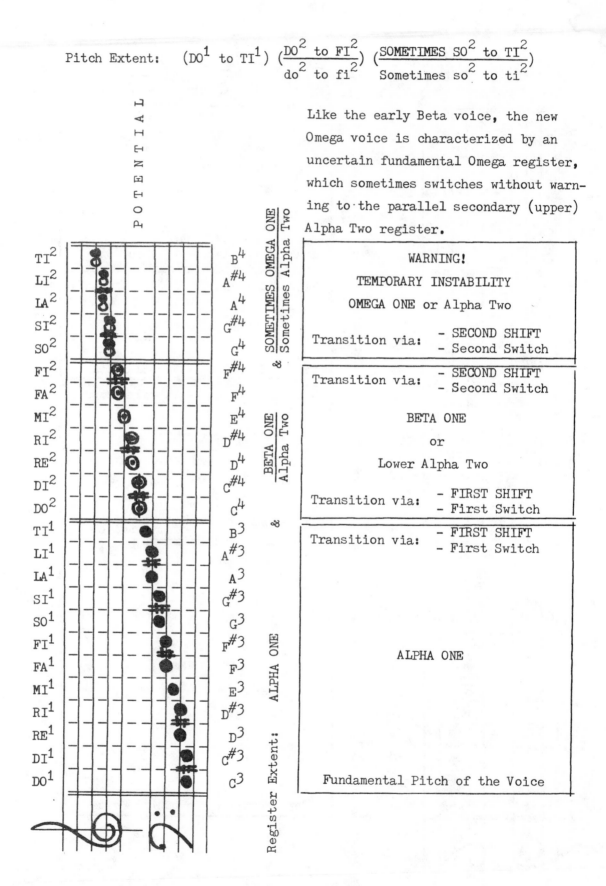

WARNING!
TEMPORARY INSTABILITY
OMEGA ONE or Alpha Two
Transition via: – SECOND SHIFT / – Second Switch

Transition via: – SECOND SHIFT / – Second Switch
BETA ONE
or
Lower Alpha Two
Transition via: – FIRST SHIFT / – First Switch

Transition via: – FIRST SHIFT / – First Switch
ALPHA ONE
Fundamental Pitch of the Voice

Pitch Extent: $(DO^1$ to $TI^1)$ $(\dfrac{DO^2 \text{ to } FI^2}{do^2 \text{ to } fi^2})$ $(\dfrac{SO^2 \text{ to } TI^2}{so^2 \text{ to } ti^2})+(\dfrac{- - -}{do^3 \text{ to } fi^3})$

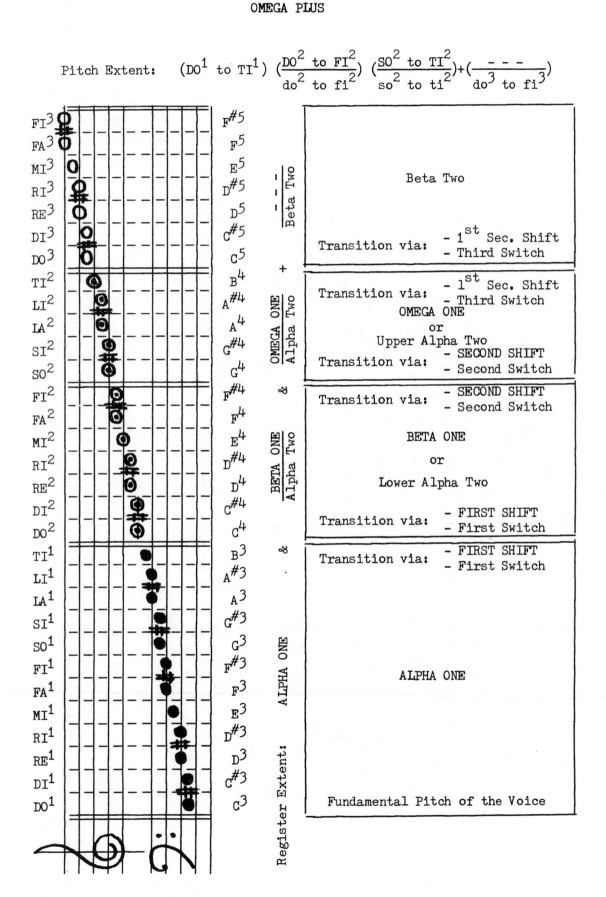

INVENTORY ITEM II
EXTENT OF REGISTRATION
INVENTORY VOCALIZATIONS

Procedural Concept: Determine the extent of registration by singing
a series of ascending vocalizations which reveal
the points of transition between registers.

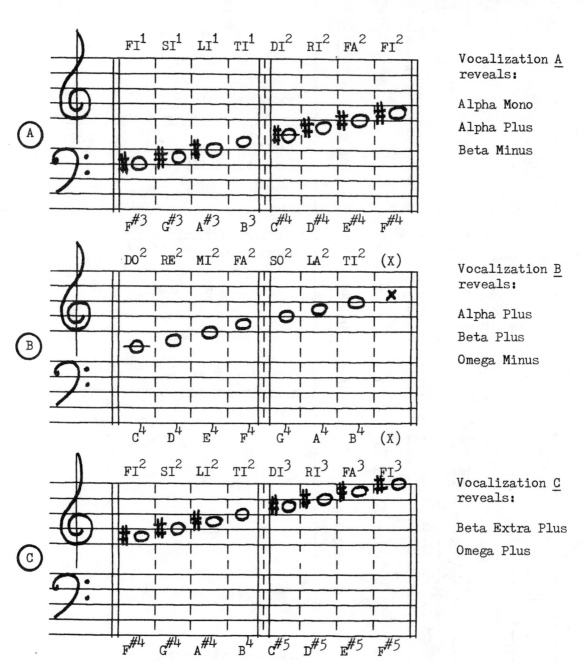

Vocalization A
reveals:

Alpha Mono

Alpha Plus

Beta Minus

Vocalization B
reveals:

Alpha Plus

Beta Plus

Omega Minus

Vocalization C
reveals:

Beta Extra Plus

Omega Plus

INVENTORY ITEM II

EXTENT OF REGISTRATION

PRELIMINARY INSTRUCTIONS

TO THE SUBJECT	TO THE READER

1. "These vocalizations are designed to reveal the registers you can now sing with correct technique."

   _ _ _ _ _ _ _ _ _

   This item is prerequisite to the development of any potential range or a maintenance program for the fully developed voice.

   _ _ _ _ _ _ _ _ _

2. "Sing these vocalizations in the same general way you sang the Item I Vocalization, especially with regard to posture."

   _ _ _ _ _ _ _ _ _

   Maintain close observation of the subject, using all indicators.

   _ _ _ _ _ _ _ _ _

3. "All pitch changes must be made without posture change."

   _ _ _ _ _ _ _ _ _

   All register transition must be negotiated by the intrinsic muscular system of the larynx.

   _ _ _ _ _ _ _ _ _

4. "Sing the vocalizations as smoothly as possible .... maintaining a slow tempo .... with moderate loudness .... on the vowel 'AH' (or the previously selected and approved alternate vowel).

   _ _ _ _ _ _ _ _ _

   LEGATO

   LENTO

   MEZZO PIANO

   MONO-VOWELIC

   _ _ _ _ _ _ _ _ _

5. "Sing each of the vocalizations on one breath."

   _ _ _ _ _ _ _ _ _

   Transition must not be rendered obscure by repeated attack.

   _ _ _ _ _ _ _ _ _

6. "We will repeat each vocalization several times if necessary."

   _ _ _ _ _ _ _ _ _

   Repeat the vocalization until the subject has followed all instructions to the letter.

   _ _ _ _ _ _ _ _ _

6. "Sing full voice unless I ask specifically for falsetto."

   When the subject is unable to sing a portion of the vocalization in fundamental voice, ask for secondary voice.

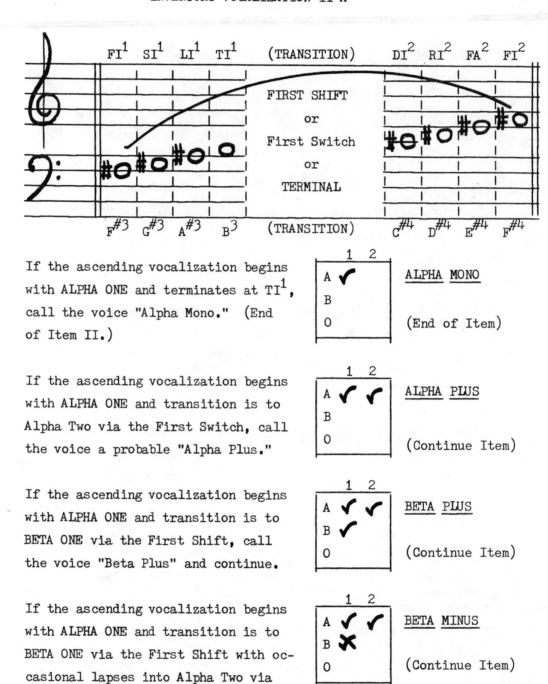

If the ascending vocalization begins with ALPHA ONE and terminates at TI^1, call the voice "Alpha Mono." (End of Item II.)

ALPHA MONO

(End of Item)

If the ascending vocalization begins with ALPHA ONE and transition is to Alpha Two via the First Switch, call the voice a probable "Alpha Plus."

ALPHA PLUS

(Continue Item)

If the ascending vocalization begins with ALPHA ONE and transition is to BETA ONE via the First Shift, call the voice "Beta Plus" and continue.

BETA PLUS

(Continue Item)

If the ascending vocalization begins with ALPHA ONE and transition is to BETA ONE via the First Shift with occasional lapses into Alpha Two via the First Switch, call the voice "Beta Minus." Continue to Vocalization II-B to inventory Upper Alpha Two.

BETA MINUS

(Continue Item)

INVENTORY ITEM II
EXTENT OF REGISTRATION
"CHECKPOINT II-A"

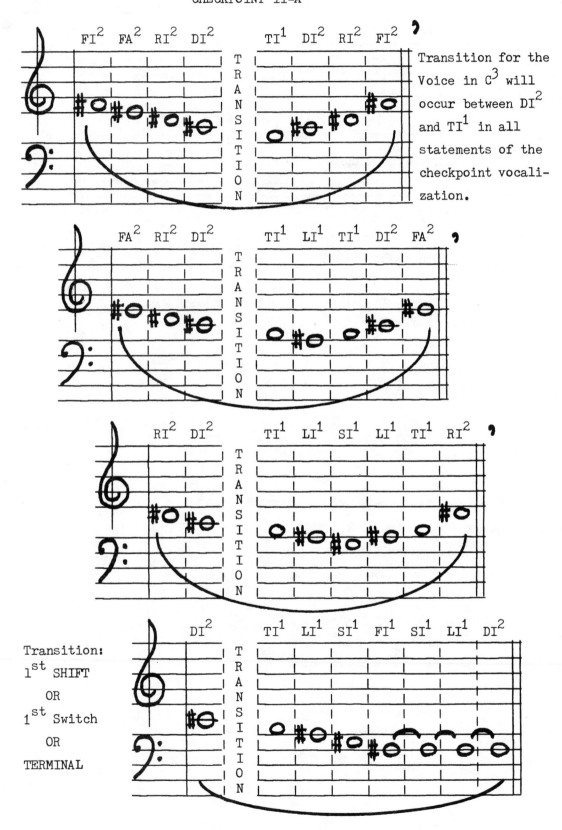

Transition for the Voice in C^3 will occur between DI^2 and TI^1 in all statements of the checkpoint vocalization.

Transition:
1st SHIFT
OR
1st Switch
OR
TERMINAL

INVENTORY ITEM II

EXTENT OF REGISTRATION

INVENTORY VOCALIZATION II-B

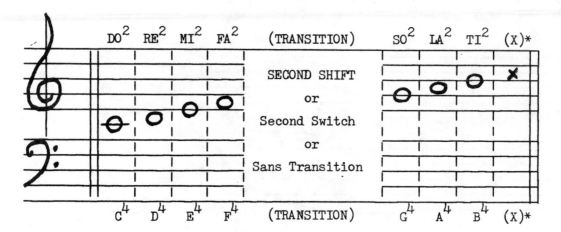

If the ascending vocalization begins with Alpha Two and continues <u>sans transition</u> to it's upper terminal Ti^2, call the voice "Alpha Plus."

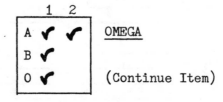

If the ascending vocalization begins with BETA ONE and transition is to Upper Alpha Two via the Second Switch, call the voice "Beta Plus" and continue.

If the ascending vocalization begins with BETA ONE and transition is to OMEGA ONE via the Second Shift, call the voice "Omega" and continue.

If the ascending vocalization begins with BETA ONE and transition is to OMEGA ONE via the Second Shift with occasional lapses into Upper Alpha Two via the Second Switch, call the voice "Omega Minus" and continue.

*Tacit extra-register pitch.

EXTENT OF REGISTRATION

"CHECKPOINT II-B"

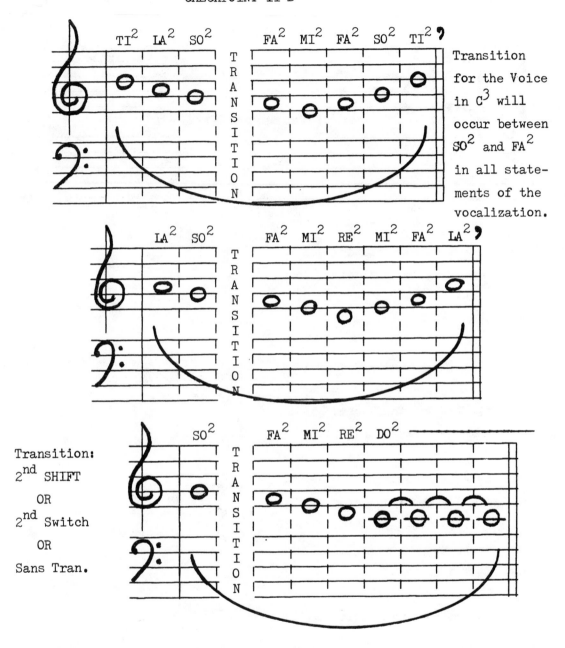

Transition
for the Voice
in c^3 will
occur between
SO^2 and FA^2
in all state-
ments of the
vocalization.

Transition:
2nd SHIFT
OR
2nd Switch
OR
Sans Tran.

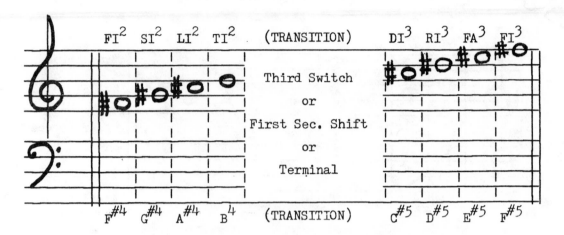

If the ascending vocalization begins with Upper Alpha Two and terminates at ti^2, call the voice "Beta Plus." End of Item II.

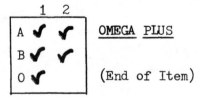

BETA PLUS

(End of Item)

If the ascending vocalization begins with Upper Alpha Two and transition is to Beta Two via the Second Shift, call the voice "Beta Extra Plus".

BETA EXTRA PLUS

(End of Item)

If the ascending vocalization begins with OMEGA ONE and terminates at TI^2, call the voice "Omega." (Not listed as or considered to be a significant phase of development.)

OMEGA

(End of Item)

If the ascending vocalization begins with OMEGA ONE and transition is to Beta Two via the Third Switch, call the voice "Omega Plus," the fully developed voice.

OMEGA PLUS

(End of Item)

INVENTORY ITEM II

EXTENT OF REGISTRATION

"CHECKPOINT II-C"

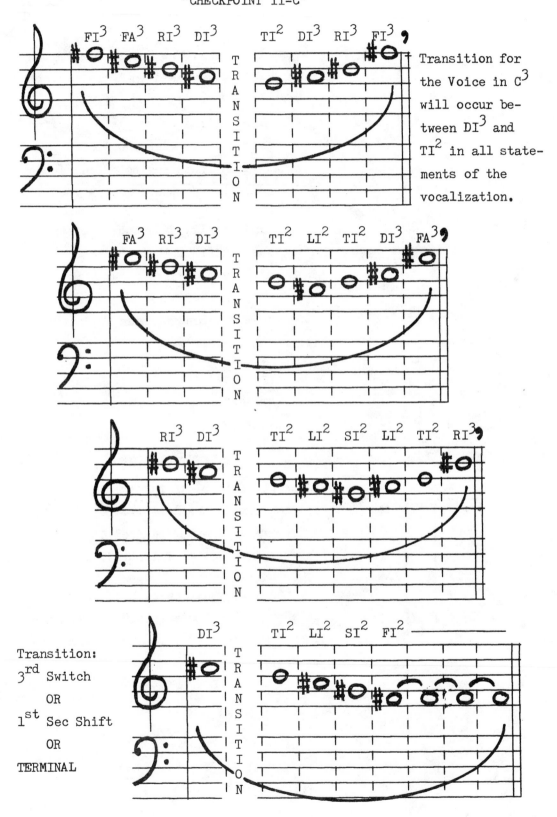

Transition for the Voice in C^3 will occur between DI^3 and TI^2 in all statements of the vocalization.

Transition:
3rd Switch
    OR
1st Sec Shift
    OR
TERMINAL

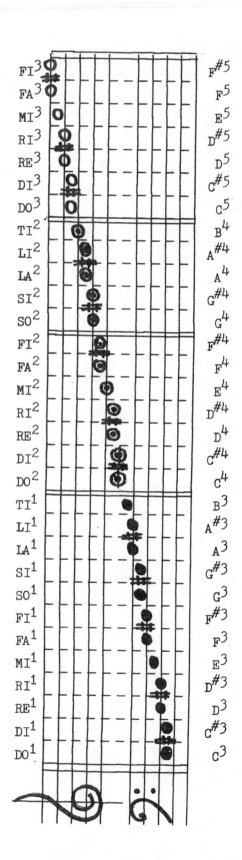

Inventory Item I, The Fundamental Pitch of the Voice, revealed that the subject possesses a Voice in C^3 which has an <u>actual</u> known Alpha One register ranging from C^3 to B^3. It also showed the <u>potential</u> pitch range and <u>potential</u> extent of registration of the Voice in C^3.

Inventory Item II, Extent of Registration, has confirmed that the Voice in C^3 is a fully developed voice with production capability of three fundamental mode and two secondary mode registers (as shown at left)....

ALPHA ONE	Alpha Two
BETA ONE	Beta Two
OMEGA ONE	

The subject enjoys an extensive pitch range of C^3 to B^4 in fundamental voice and can employ the Beta Two register to extend the range upward from C^5 to $F^{\#5}$ in secondary voice (falsetto).

Inventory Items I and II have together made possible a more specific nomenclature for voice. The Subject possesses an ....

OMEGA PLUS VOICE in C^3.

INVENTORY VOCALIZATION III

A MELODIC VOCALIZATION

INVENTORY VOCALIZATION III
A MELODIC VOCALIZATION

Inventory Vocalizations I and II were designed to reveal the pitch range and the extent of registration of the voice. There remain a few important items which must become a part of the inventory of a Credible Sing Machine. Among these are <u>vibrato</u>, basic techniques of <u>onset</u>, <u>sustain</u>, <u>legato</u>, and <u>flexibility</u>, the <u>weight</u> concept, the <u>loudness</u> concept, <u>breath</u> management, and <u>resonance</u> management.

To the taped Inventory Vocalizations I and II, add yet a third, a melodic vocalization which consists of a familiar melody which lends itself to legato singing.

The vocalization should be sung <u>a cappella</u>, <u>legato</u>, <u>mezzo piano</u>, and <u>monovowellic</u>. Instruct the subject to sing the vocalization twice, the first time breathing only at the end of each score as indicated by the usual ('), the second time breathing as well at the indicator (x).

The vocalization should be of sufficient range span to include a significant portion of each fundamental register. This necessitates a repertory of vocalizations suitable for each fundamental voice, Alpha, Beta, or Omega.

MELODIC VOCALIZATION III-ALPHA
The melodic vocalization for the Alpha Voice is restricted to a pitch range of DO^1 to TI^1.

MELODIC VOCALIZATION III-BETA
The melodic vocalization for the Beta Voice is restricted to a pitch range of DO^1 to FI^2.

MELODIC VOCALIZATION III-OMEGA
The melodic vocalization for the Omega Voice is restricted to a pitch range of DO^1 to TI^2.

MELODIC VOCALIZATION III-ALPHA
(FOR ALPHA VOICE IN C^3)

The Eighteenth Century German melody commonly known by the Samuel F.
Smith title, "My Country, 'Tis of Thee", is suitable as a melodic vocalization because of it's familiarity to most Americans, it's pitch
range of a minor seventh which permits the choice of DO^1 to LI^1 or
DI^1 to TI^1, and it's long, flowing melodic line. As Inventory Melodic
Vocalization III-Alpha for the Alpha Voice in C^3 it could be written
as follows....

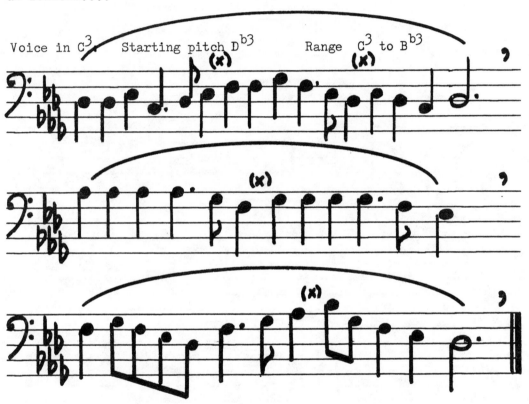

Other suitable melodic vocalizations for Alpha voice are....

Coventry Carol (15th Century English)   Minor 6th   Begin on RI^1

Aura Lee (19th Century American)   Minor 7th   Begin on DI^1

O Jesu, Sweet Child (S. Scheidt)   Minor 7th   Begin on FA^1

MELODIC VOCALIZATION III-BETA
(FOR BETA VOICE IN c^3)

The Welsh traditional melody we know as "All Thru the Night" is an excellent melodic vocalization for the Beta voice. It's scalestep line
and pitch range of a major ninth are especially good for the inventory
of basic technique and register transition.

Start on FI^1 of the voice to be inventoried. This provides a highest
pitch of RI^2 (middle of the Beta register) and a low of DI^1, ideal for
our purposes. Have the subject sing the melody twice, first breathing
only at the end of each score, then using the alternate midscore breath
indicators (X).

Voice in c^3: Starting pitch G^{b3} Range D^{b3} to E^{b4}

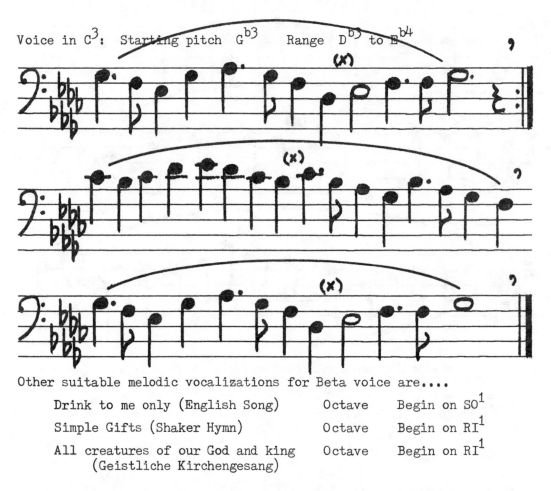

Other suitable melodic vocalizations for Beta voice are....

Drink to me only (English Song)	Octave	Begin on SO^1
Simple Gifts (Shaker Hymn)	Octave	Begin on RI^1
All creatures of our God and king (Geistliche Kirchengesang)	Octave	Begin on RI^1

Note: "My Country,'tis of Thee" can be used (for the sake of continuity)
as the Beta Vocalization, starting on FI^1.

The seventeenth century English air "Greensleeves" is appropriate for inventory of the fully registered voice because of it's pitch range of a minor tenth and it's long, flowing melodic line.

Start on SO^1 of the voice being inventoried. This requires a highest pitch of FA^2 (difficult to everextend in Beta) and a low of RE^1. Have the subject sing the melody twice, breathing as in the Beta Vocalization.

Other suitable melodic vocalizations for Omega voice are....

I Will Arise (Southern Folk)   11th   Begin on SO^1

Be Thou My Vision (Irish Traditional) 11th   Begin on FA^1

Were You There (American Spiritual)   11th   Begin on DO^1

Note: "All Thru the Night" can be used as the Omega Vocalization, starting on DO^2. This requires a range of SO^1 to LA^2.

THE CREDIBLE SING MACHINE

POSTINVENTORY

THE CREDIBLE SING MACHINE
POSTINVENTORY

The concomitant items which follow the actual inventory compose the Postinventory of the Credible Sing Machine. This section of the inventory can be conducted in the solitude of your retreat, requiring only the tape of the inventory and a reasonably accurate tape player, and enhanced by a comfortable chair, adequate lighting, and perhaps the beverage of your choice (in my case ALWAYS freshly ground Celebes Kalossi coffee).

The postinventory should be taken as soon as possible after the completion of the actual inventory. Although the predominate indicator to the postinventory items will be the Aural Indicator, a fresh recall of the actual inventory will be helpful, especially in terms of the postures for breath and resonance.

Perhaps a preliminary review of the pertinant sections of " The Vocalist as Voice Manager" is in order (See The Credible Sing Machine). Do not despair if first efforts are less than excellent. With experience you can become fluent, so that every sound reveals the function. We will consider the following items:

III. Vibrato
IV. Basic Technique
   A. Onset
   B. Sustain
   C. Legato
V. Weight
VI. Loudness
VII. Breath Management
VIII. Resonance Management

VIBRATO: ∿∿∿ ☐ ～～～ ☐ ∿ᐯᐯ ☐ ——— ☐

The inventory vocalizations revealed that the pulse character of the Subject's voice can be catagorized generally as (choose one):

Normalized. The normalized pulse is indicative of well-limited production. It's production is free of vocal cord hypercompression and exhibits regularity, maximal quality, and appropriate rate and extent.

Restrained. The restrained pulse reflects a degree of overextension. The resultant hypercompression diminishes regularity and can retard rate, increase extent, and reduce quality.

Tremulous. The tremulous pulse is a characteristic of the severely overtaxed voice and is heard as irregular, spasmodic, wobbly, or erratic, with reduced rate and/or increased extent. Hypercompressed production requires increased power for onset, which magnifies the problem.

Suppressed. The suppressed pulse is the indicator of the unprotected, non-pulsate voice. The "straight" voice of little or no pulse is effective only in severely limited range of combined pitch, quality and loudness. Stamina is lacking and longevity becomes "short-gevity."

INVENTORY ITEM IV
BASIC TECHNIQUE

Voice management in the most basic sense has to do with the manner in which we start, continue and connect pitches of varying degrees
of weight, loudness and compression.

Start. Although the start of the voice has been traditionally
called the "attack", I stand with those who prefer the "onset" as a
perhaps more gentle alternative.

Continue. To continue on the same pitch has been referred to
without discord as the "sustain".

Connect. The standard term for the connection of a series of
different pitches will continue as the "legato".

The Basic Technique category is preceeded by that of Vibrato because of the absolute necessity of adherence to this neural pulse
which activates the shock absorption system of the voice. (See The
Credible Sing Machine: How It Works, "Pulsation System", page 37
and "Within the Combined Limits: Vibrato", page 57)

The Basic Technique category is presented in three subdivisions:

INVENTORY ITEM IV-A   BASIC TECHNIQUE: ONSET

INVENTORY ITEM IV-B   BASIC TECHNIQUE: SUSTAIN

INVENTORY ITEM IV-C   BASIC TECHNIQUE: LEGATO

INVENTORY ITEM IV-A

BASIC TECHNIQUE: ONSET

ONSET:	Appropriate ☐	PULSE CHARACTERISTICS:	∼∼∼ ☐
	Aspirate ☐		∿∿ ☐
	Hard ☐		⌇⌇ ☐
			▬▬ ☐

The inventory vocalizations revealed that the Subject's voice was started with a detectable mode of compression which affected the character of the pulsate voice.

APPROPRIATE ☑

Appropriate onset. The start of the Subject's voice was accomplished with moderate compression of the vocal cords and was initially pulsate.

ASPIRATE ☑

Aspirate onset. The start of the Subject's voice was preceeded by the noise of wasted breath as air pressure was increased prior to the adduction (bringing together of the vocal cords) process. (Aspirate onset, hypo-compression, is often continued as hyper-compression.)

HARD ☑

Hard onset. The start of the Subject's voice was typical of overextended production, characterized by reduced quality and restrained, tremulous, or suppressed pulse.

Pulse characteristics. See Inventory Item III, Vibrato.

NORMALIZED   ∼∼∼

RESTRAINED   ∿∿

TREMULOUS   ⌇⌇

SUPPRESSED   ▬▬

INVENTORY ITEM IV-B

BASIC TECHNIQUE: SUSTAIN

SUSTAIN:	Appropriate ☐	PULSE CHARACTERISTICS:	〜〜 ☐
	Aspirate ☐		〰 ☐
	Hard ☐		⌇ ☐
			— ☐

The inventory vocalizations revealed that the Subject's voice, once set in motion (see "onset"), was continued with a detectable mode of compression and related pulse characteristics.

APPROPRIATE ☑

Appropriate sustain. The continuation of the Subject's voice (same pitch) was accomplished with moderate compression and appropriate pulse.

ASPIRATE ☑

Aspirate sustain. The continuation of the Subject's voice (same pitch) was accomplished with incompletely closed vocal cords. This hypo-compressed production was accompanied by the noise of wasted breath.

HARD ☑

Hard sustain. The continuation of the Subject's voice (same pitch) was accomplished with tightly closed vocal cords. This hyper-compressed production can be accompanied by breathiness.

Pulse characteristics.
Normalized.   〜〜〜
Restrained.   〰
Tremulous.   ⌇
Suppressed.   —

INVENTORY ITEM IV-C

BASIC TECHNIQUE: LEGATO

LEGATO:	Efficient	☐	PULSE CHARACTERISTICS:	〜〜〜	☐
	Sporadic	☐		～	☐
	Disconnected	☐		⩘	☐
				▬▬	☐

The inventory vocalizations revealed that the Subject's voice effected the connection of a series of different pitches with a discernable degree of adherence to the pulse of the voice.

EFFICIENT ☑

Efficient legato. The Subject was able to connect a series of different pitches with a high degree of vibrato efficiency.

SPORADIC ☑

Sporadic legato. The Subject was able to connect a series of different pitches, but was inconsistent in maintaining the vibrato, especially in the more rapidly changing progressions.

DISCONNECTED ☑

Disconnected (non-legato). The Subject was unable to negotiate a pulsate connection of a series of different pitches.

Pulse characteristics.
Normalized. 〜〜〜
Restrained. ～
Tremulous. ⩘
Suppressed. ▬▬

INVENTORY ITEM V
WEIGHT

```
┌──────────────────────────────────────────────────────┐
│        OPTIMAL     ● │ │ │ │ │ │ │ │ │ │ │ │ │ │      │
│ WEIGHT:   ┌───────────────────────────────────────┐   │
│           │ Lightest        Moderate      Heaviest │   │
│        HABITUAL └─────────────●─────────────────────┘  │
│ (Place indicator ● at appropriate points of optimal and habitual) │
└──────────────────────────────────────────────────────┘
```

The inventory vocalizations revealed that the Subject's weight concept, that is, his understanding of ·the optimal weight of his voice, was incorrect. The HABITUAL weight indicator shows a heavier concept than is the correct OPTIMAL (as assessed through inventory).

OPTIMAL WEIGHT

A comparison with the known weight range of other voices of similar pitch revealed that the Subject's optimal weight was significantly on the light side of the scale. The Subject's voice can be described as a moderately light (or mezzo lyric) voice in c^3. (See The Credible Sing Machine: How It Works, "Within the Weight Limit," page 52)

HABITUAL WEIGHT

The inventory vocalizations revealed that the Subject's voice was habitually overweighted and thus was inventoried as being used with moderate weight. The deviation from the "moderately light" designation is slight, but can be a significant deterrent to voice longevity. (See The Credible Sing Machine: How It Works, "Without the Weight Limit," page 53)

RECOMMENDED NOMENCLATURE

Light	=	Lyric
Medium	=	Mezzo
Heavy	=	Dramatic

	P	M	F	Alpha One
LOUDNESS: (Circle one for each register)	P	M	F	Beta One
	P	M	F	Omega One

The inventory vocalization, when repeated at different degrees of loudness, revealed the loudness range of the Subject's voice and provided the means for assessing the distribution of register loudness range. (Suggested sequence: M - P - F)

The Subject was capable of singing quietly in the register indicated by the circled "P". The PIANO register has a severely limited range of loudness.

The Subject was capable of singing moderately loud in the register indicated by the circled "M". The MEZZO register has a moderate range of loudness.

The Subject was capable of powerful singing in the register indicated by the circled "F". The FORTE register has an extensive range of loudness.

Note: Each degree of loudness must be achieved with a clear, unforced production.

INVENTORY ITEM VII

BREATH MANAGEMENT

BREATH MANAGEMENT:	Maximal line (x) ☐	Appropriate posture ☐
		Shoulder fault ☐
	Minimal line (') ☐	Rib cage fault ☐
		Abdominal fault ☐

The inventory vocalization revealed characteristics of the subject's breath management in terms of length of line capability and posture.

(') ☑ **Maximal length line.** The Subject was able to sing long phrases as indicated by the sign (').

(x) ☑ **Minimal length line.** The Subject was able to sing only short phrases as indicated by the sign (x).

APPROPRIATE POSTURE ☑ **Appropriate posture.** The Subject maintained a high rib cage posture. Expansion just below the rib cage area indicated substantial abdominal support.

SHOULDER FAULT ☑ **Shoulder fault.** The Subject's shoulders were inordinately raised during inhalation and maintained in high position.

RIB CAGE FAULT ☑ **Rib cage fault.** The Subject's rib cage posture was inordinately low. This was observable as an upward movement occurring with each inhalation. This fault is often accompanied by a protruded jaw.

ABDOMINAL FAULT ☑ **Abdominal fault.** The Subject's abdominal support was lacking. This was observable as an absence of expansion below the area of the rib cage.

INVENTORY ITEM VIII

RESONANCE MANAGEMENT

RESONANCE: Appropriate ☐   POSTURE:  ☐
                                                          ☐
             Hyper-nasal ☐    ☐

The inventory vocalizations revealed the resonance management of the Subject's voice in terms of it's mode of resonance and related observable postures.

Appropriate resonance. The Subject sang with oral resonance, free from nasal resonance.

Hyper-nasal resonance. The Subject's resonance was composed of oral resonance mixed with a substantial measure of nasal resonance.

Appropriate posture. The Subject's jaw was in a moderate position, neither protruded or retracted.

Thrust fault. The Subject's jaw was protruded. This can activate the muscular connection between palate and larnyx to partially open the nasal passages and create hyper-nasal resonance.

Retraction fault. The Subject's jaw was retracted. This can alter the shape of the resonance passage and effect a resonance change.

THE CREDIBLE SING MACHINE

DIAGNOSTIC REPORT

THE CREDIBLE SING MACHINE
DIAGNOSTIC REPORT

The pre-inventory phase provided a chronology of significant vocal events in terms of activity and dysfunction.

The inventory proper introduced a series of vocalizations which facilitated the gathering of comprehensive specific information about the Subject's voice including not only the present voice limits, but the potential limits.

The post-inventory phase provided for the acquisition of additional information through the study of the taped inventory procedures.

The diagnostic report will be based on a synthesization of all the aforementioned data which permits the assignment of the Subject to a

CATEGORY OF TRAINING.

THE CREDIBLE SING MACHINE PREINVENTORY
CHRONOLOGY OF VOCAL ACTIVITY

Name: First   Last

Date of Chronology

0 Birthdate [＿＿＿＿＿]   Birthplace [＿＿＿＿＿＿＿＿＿]

1

2

3

4

5

6

7   1   (SEE "PREINVENTORY", PAGE 4)

8   2

9   3
                         (ENTER SIGNIFICANT VOCAL ACTIVITY
10 4   ON "DIAGNOSTIC REPORT, PART ONE,"
                         PAGE 70. RETAIN THIS FORM IN
11 5   SINGER'S ACTIVE FOLDER OR FILE,
                         AS APPROPRIATE.)
12 6

13 7

14 8

15 9

16 10

17 11

18 12

19 C1

20 C2

21 C3

22 C4

THE CREDIBLE SING MACHINE PREINVENTORY
CHRONOLOGY OF VOCAL DYSFUNCTION

Name: First   Last

Date of Chronology

0   Birthdate [   ] Birthplace [   ]

1

2

3

4

5

6

7   1   (SEE "PREINVENTORY," PAGE 5)

8   2

9   3
                          (ENTER SIGNIFICANT VOCAL DYSFUNCTION
10   4   ON "DIAGNOSTIC REPORT, PART ONE,"
                          PAGE 70. RETAIN THIS FORM IN
11   5   SINGER'S ACTIVE FOLDER OR FILE,
                          AS APPROPRIATE.)
12   6

13   7

14   8

15   9

16 10

17 11

18 12

19 C1

20 C2

21 C3

22 C4

Name: First   Second   Last   Age   Date of Inventory

I.   FUNDAMENTAL PITCH OF THE VOICE: (DO^1) ☐

II. EXTENT OF REGISTRATION: ALPHA ONE ☐   BETA ONE ☐   OMEGA ONE ☐
         Alpha Two ☐   Beta Two ☐

III. VIBRATO: 〰️ ☐   ～ ☐   〰 ☐   — ☐

IV-A ONSET:
   Appropriate ☐   PULSE CHARACTERISTICS: 〰️ ☐
   Aspirate ☐   ～ ☐
   Hard ☐   〰 ☐
                                                   — ☐

IV-B SUSTAIN:
   Appropriate ☐   PULSE CHARACTERISTICS: 〰️ ☐
   Aspirate ☐   ～ ☐
   Hard ☐   〰 ☐
                                                   — ☐

IV-C LEGATO:
   Efficient ☐   PULSE CHARACTERISTICS: 〰️ ☐
   Sporadic ☐   ～ ☐
   Disconnected ☐   〰 ☐
                                                   — ☐

V.   WEIGHT: OPTIMAL
         Lightest   Moderate   Heaviest
         HABITUAL

VI. LOUDNESS: P M F   ALPHA ONE
                          P M F   BETA ONE
                          P M F   OMEGA ONE

VII. BREATH MANAGEMENT:
   Maximal line (') ☐   Appropriate posture ☐
                             Shoulder fault ☐
   Minimal line (x) ☐   Rib cage fault ☐
                             Abdominal fault ☐

VIII. RESONANCE MANAGEMENT:
   Appropriate ☐   POSTURE: ☐
                                     ☐
   Hyper-nasal ☐   ☐

(TRANSCRIBE TO "DIAGNOSTIC REPORT, PART ONE", PAGE 70, WITH APPROPRIATE
ANNOTATION.)

70

THE CREDIBLE SING MACHINE DIAGNOSTIC REPORT, PART ONE

Name: First   Second   Last   Age   Date of Inventory

SIGNIFICANT VOCAL ACTIVITY

(FROM "CHRONOLOGY OF VOCAL ACTIVITY", PAGE 67)

SIGNIFICANT VOCAL DYSFUNCTION

(FROM "CHRONOLOGY OF VOCAL DYSFUNCTION", PAGE 68)

SUMMARY OF INVENTORY

Fundamental Pitch: _____

Extent of Registration: _____

Vibrato: _____

Onset: _____

Sustain: _____

Legato: _____ (FROM "INVENTORY", PAGE 69)

Weight: _____

Loudness: _____

Breath Management: _____

Resonance Management: _____

Other: _____

PHASE OF DEVELOPMENT:	ALPHA ☐	BETA ☐	OMEGA ☐
	Minus ☐	Minus ☐	Minus ☐
	Mono ☐	Plus ☐	Plus ☐
	Plus ☐	Extra ☐	

The Phase of Development of the Subject's voice was revealed by Inventory Item II, "Extent of Registration." It is a prerequisite to the assignment of a developmental program.

ALPHA ☑ Alpha. The Subject has a one-register voice . . . .

Minus ☑ Minus some pitches in the upper part of the register.

Mono ☑ Mono(modal) in that the voice is limited to full voice only.

Plus ☑ Plus one falsetto register which extends the upper range.

BETA ☑ Beta. The Subject has a two-register voice . . . .

Minus ☑ Minus stability in the pitches of the Beta register.

Plus ☑ Plus one falsetto register which extends the upper range.

Extra ☑ Extra range from a second falsetto register.

OMEGA ☑ Omega. The Subject has a three-register voice . . . .

Minus ☑ Minus stability in the pitches of the Omega register.

Plus ☑ Plus additional range from a second falsetto register.

CATEGORY OF FUNCTION

```
┌────────────────────────────────────────────────────────────────┐
│                                               Breathy  ☐         │
│                                               Harsh    ☐         │
│  CATEGORY OF FUNCTION:        Clear  ☐                           │
│                                               Hoarse   ☐         │
│                                               Aphonic  ☐         │
└────────────────────────────────────────────────────────────────┘
```

The condition or category of function of the Subject's voice was revealed by indicators of function. (See The Credible Sing Machine: How It Works, "Function Without the Limit. An Insidious Progression: Dysfunction to Pathology.")

CLEAR   ☑   Clear. The Subject's voice was produced with ease and efficiency.

BREATHY   ☑   Breathy. The Subject's voice was accompanied by the noise of unvocalized air, the result of hyperactivity.

HARSH   ☑   Harsh. The Subject's voice was forced, the result of hypercompression to eliminate breathiness.

HOARSE   ☑   Hoarse. The Subject's voice was both harsh and breathy, the danger sign of tissue alteration, pathology.

APHONIC   ☑   Aphonic. The Subject was unable to sing or speak.

CATEGORY OF TRAINING

CATEGORY OF TRAINING:	Maintenance	☐
	Development	☐
(Medical Evaluation Required)	Rehabituation	☐
(Medical Evaluation Required)	Pathology	☐

The total inventory of the Subject's voice has revealed an appropriate Category of Training.

MAINTENANCE ✓ Maintenance. The Subject has a fully developed voice in Clear category of function. Implement total "Day of the Singer" program. (See page 75)

DEVELOPMENT ✓ Development. The Subject has an under-registered voice in Clear category of function. Implement modified "Day of the Singer" program.

REHABITUATION ✓ Rehabituation. The Subject has a voice in Breathy, Harsh, or Hoarse category of function. Medical evaluation is prerequisite to assignment. After examination reveals no pathology (tissue alteration) implement modified "Day of the Singer" program to eliminate abusive habits and effect rehabituation.

PATHOLOGY ✓ Pathology. Medical evaluation revealed that the Subject possessed a pathology of the vocal system. During the period of voice rest as an alternative to surgury, or voice rest during the post-surgical period, provide information as a preliminary to training. After voice rest, implement modified "Day of the Singer" program in Rehabituation category.

Name: First   Second   Last   Age   Date of Inventory

PHASE OF DEVELOPMENT:

ALPHA	☐	BETA	☐	OMEGA	☐
Minus	☐	Minus	☐	Minus	☐
Mono	☐	Plus	☐	Plus	☐
Plus	☐	Extra	☐		☐

(FROM PAGE 67)

CATEGORY OF FUNCTION: Clear ☐

(FROM PAGE 68)

Breathy	☐
Harsh	☐
Hoarse	☐
Aphonic	☐

CATEGORY OF TRAINING:
            (Medical Evaluation Required)
(FROM PAGE 69)   (Medical Evaluation Required)

Maintenance	☐
Development	☐
Rehabituation	☐
Pathology	☐

MEDICAL EVALUATION

Date of Evaluation: _____

Physician and Specialty: _____

(   )   Name: First   Second   Last   Specialty
_____   _____
   Office Phone   Address

Diagnosis: _____

_____

Examination: _____
            (SEE "CATEGORY OF TRAINING", PAGE 69)

Causal Diagnosis: _____

_____

Treatment: _____

_____

Prognosis: _____

_____

PRESCRIPTION

FOR THE WELL-INVENTORIED CREDIBLE SING MACHINE

The past has been reviewed.... the present limits have been described.... the future or potential limits have been projected. The
phase of development has been noted.... the category of function revealed.... Medical evaluation if required has been accomplished....
a category of training has been prescribed.

The training concept of the Credible Sing Machine, "The Day of
the Singer", is a comprehensive conditioning program for voice. It
seeks to fulfill the physiological viewpoint that certain behaviours
must occur with regularity if the voice is to prosper (Review The
Credible Sing Machine: How It Works, "The Vocalist as Voice Manager").

THE DAY OF THE SINGER

The Singer must each day decide whether or not to sing,
and if so, how much to sing.

The Singer must warm up the voice in a systematic manner, regularly and before every extensive use.

The Singer must elect literature which is appropriate
for the combined limits of the voice (Pitch, Weight, Loudness).

The Singer must select vocalizations which, when added
to the warmups and literature, provide for the utilization
of the total voice in appropriate measure.

The Singer must respond appropriately to indicators of
fatigue.

The Day of the Singer is presented in the third volume of the
Credible Sing Machine series,

HOW TO TRAIN THE CREDIBLE SING MACHINE